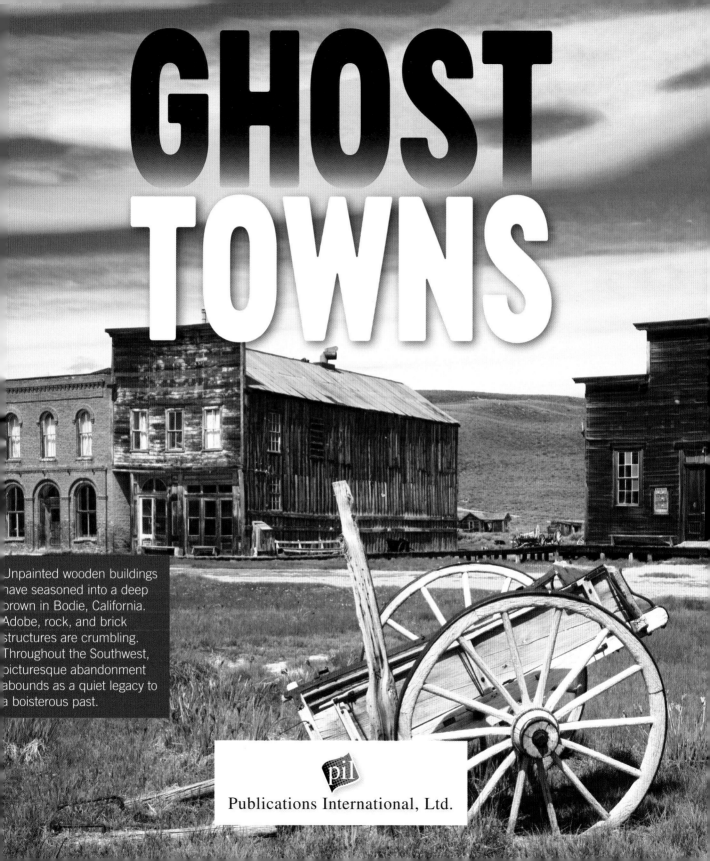

# GHOST TOWNS

Unpainted wooden buildings have seasoned into a deep brown in Bodie, California. Adobe, rock, and brick structures are crumbling. Throughout the Southwest, picturesque abandonment abounds as a quiet legacy to a boisterous past.

pil

Publications International, Ltd.

Contributing writer: Gary B. Speck

Facts verified by Marty Strasen

**Let's get social!**

[instagram] @Publications_International
[facebook] @PublicationsInternational
**www.pilbooks.com**

# TABLE OF CONTENTS

# THE SOUTHWESTERN STATES

Explorers and pioneers pushing against the edges of settlement discovered gold, silver, and other precious minerals in scattered areas across the American Southwest. Towns such as Bodie, California, grew quickly and were then abandoned once mine production dipped below the profitability line. When these communities died, people left behind their withered hopes and faded dreams. What remains today are weather-worn schools, churches, businesses, and homes.

**In a very measured understatement during his State of the Union address on December 5, 1848, President James K. Polk tossed kindling in the flames of the burgeoning case of worldwide gold fever.**

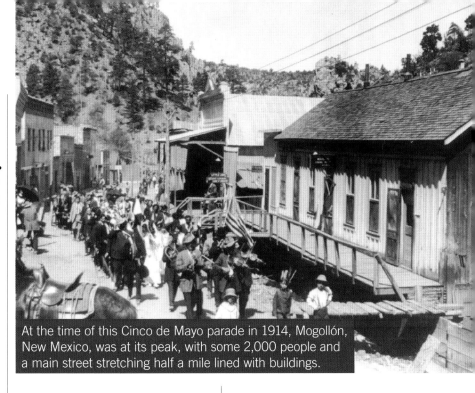

At the time of this Cinco de Mayo parade in 1914, Mogollón, New Mexico, was at its peak, with some 2,000 people and a main street stretching half a mile lined with buildings.

"The accounts of the abundance of gold in that territory are of such an extraordinary character as would scarcely command belief were they not corroborated by the authentic reports of officers in the public service who have visited the mineral district and derived the facts which they detail from personal observation.

"Nearly the whole of the male population of the country have gone to the gold districts. Ships arriving on the coast are deserted by their crews and their voyages suspended for want of sailors."

Newspapers splashed golden headlines to the far corners of the earth— the California Gold Rush was under way. In a five-year span, some 300,000 argonauts from all over the world descended upon the soon to become "Golden State."

### Gold Fever!

From 1848 to 1853, the rush for gold was in full boom. Lots of gold was found—some 12 million ounces, worth multiple billions in today's dollars. The once-pastoral western landscape was converted into teeming clusters of temporary mining camps and transitory towns with little thought given to permanence. Once the riches were stripped from the rivers, the miners moved on, leaving behind remains of the ephemeral camps and towns, the people taking only what they could carry or toss into a wagon or on the back of a mule or horse.

In what barely seemed any time at all, California's rivers had given up their treasure, and the easy diggings were gone. The gold mining industry itself, however, was firmly entrenched as less people-intensive hydraulic and hard-rock mining took over. Many of the original argonauts morphed into prospectors, now spreading east and north across the West looking for the next boom. New discoveries were made. And new mining rushes ensued.

Outside the original gold mining region in California, prospectors combed the Great Basin, the deserts, and even the Rocky Mountain forests in Nevada, Utah, Colorado, Arizona, New Mexico—all the way to Texas—in search of golden wealth. And gold was found. So were silver, copper, and a plethora of other valuable minerals. Towns boomed and busted. The prospectors then moved on to the next "Big Thing." This was a cycle that

The aroma of fresh-baked pies has been replaced by the dusty smell of well-seasoned wood in Animas Forks, Colorado. Mournful breezes blow where the joyful sounds of children playing once echoed through this vacant home in the Southwestern mountains. Dead window sockets glare eerily where glassed-in windows once glowed with warmth. One hundred years ago, this house was alive. Today, it is a rickety skeleton of the past.

repeated over and over and over again. Where viable communities remained, agriculture, transportation, and government followed. Mining opened up the American Southwest, creating the vast majority of the thousands of towns scattered across the region's landscape. Rising and ebbing across the economic landscape, farming, cattle, logging, and railroad building also tossed in their contributions, as did tourism and the military.

## Abandoned to the Elements

Today, most of these towns are gone or empty—at best,

**ABOVE** Visions of wealth drove prospectors across the region's mountains and deserts in search of gold, silver, and other valuable mineral deposits. When pay dirt was found, as it was in Silver City, Utah (pictured), the discoveries were often quickly followed by a rush of people, all looking to cash in on the find. Saloon owners, teamsters, hoteliers, blacksmiths, storekeepers, and people of many legitimate (as well as nefarious) trades converged on the site, slapping together an instant town.

they are mere shells of what they once had been. Ghost towns, they are barren or rubbled sites with a few foundation outlines, crumbled piles of rock, or melted adobe walls. Some—such as Belmont, Nevada; Chloride, New Mexico; and Darwin, California—have a smattering of ruins, abandoned buildings, and a small resident population. Others have survived and are still living, although not thriving. The population of places such as Randsburg, California; Nevadaville, Colorado; and Oatman, Arizona, is much lower than during their boom days. A select few towns such as Bisbee, Arizona, and Silverton, Colorado, remain viable communities and the seats of their respective counties. Even so, population levels are far below what they had been in the boom years, and these communities are filled with historic structures.

Because most of the land in the Southwest is dry, aridity has preserved the majority of structures. Government ownership of many towns hasn't created an economic reason to tear down unused buildings (the government doesn't pay property taxes to itself). The American Southwest is truly a place where well-preserved ghost

**BELOW** The squat, concrete jail at the west end of town still greets visitors to Randsburg, California. Inside its single cell, a display shows what life "on the inside" was like for those unfortunate enough to sample its hospitality.

towns still give travelers a glimpse of the past.

The rugged landscape of the American West can inspire conflicting emotions. This is the land where a little girl was supposedly overheard praying, "Good-bye God, I'm going to Bodie." Of course, the Bodie newspaper refuted that, claiming she was misquoted. The quote should have read, "Good. By God, I'm going to Bodie." The West is where Billy the Kid, Black Bart, the Earp brothers, Mark Twain, and hundreds of legendary characters roamed—good, bad, and in-between. It is the land of 20-mule teams, Wells Fargo and Company stagecoaches, and Route 66.

In this land of vast horizons, sagebrush, and majestic scenery, thousands of ghost towns are eager to share their stories.

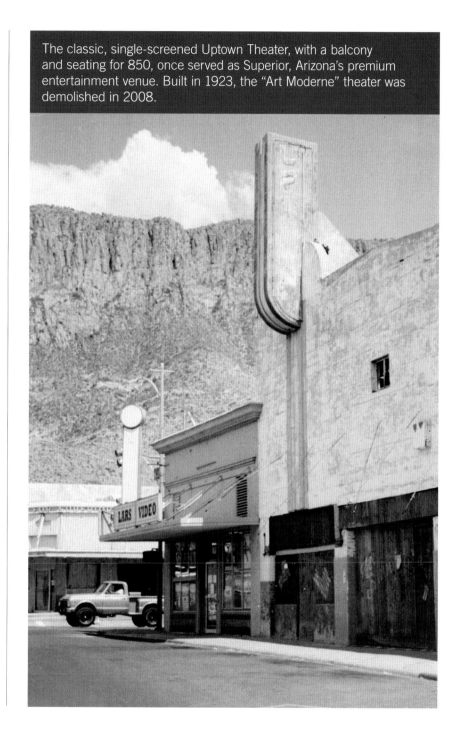

The classic, single-screened Uptown Theater, with a balcony and seating for 850, once served as Superior, Arizona's premium entertainment venue. Built in 1923, the "Art Moderne" theater was demolished in 2008.

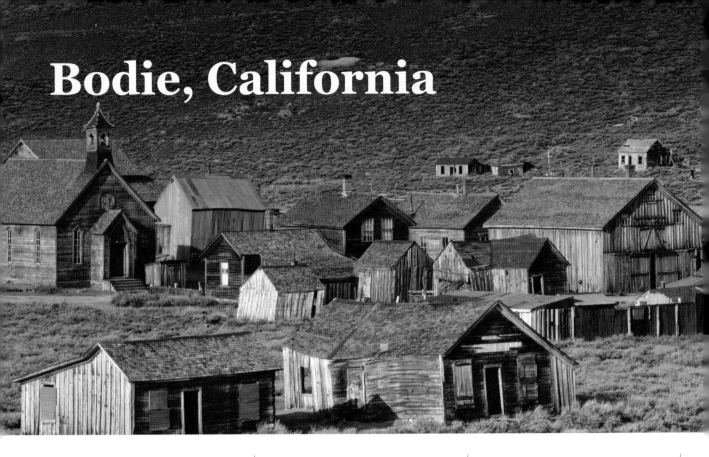

# Bodie, California

**Y**esterday's Bodie was a true boomtown filled with a couple thousand wooden buildings and as many as 10,000 people milling through its bustling streets. Today's Bodie is a state historic park, a gaunt skeleton of what once was: the best-known, most-written about, and most-photographed ghost town in America. Killings were a daily occurrence, and "The Bad Man from Bodie" became legend.

Waterman S. (Bill) Bodey discovered gold east of the Sierras and north of Mono Lake in 1859. He perished in a snowstorm that winter, but a small, quiet mining camp named after him developed at the discovery site. The peacefulness changed in 1875, however, with the exposure of a massive, rich pocket of gold deep in one of the mines. Bodie became the place to be and went from quiet to rough, uncultured, and uncivilized overnight. By 1877 the mile-long main street was solidly lined with businesses, including 65 saloons. In 1881, a local pastor called Bodie "a sea of sin, lashed by the tempests of lust and passion."

More than a century of horrid winters, a pair of major fires, and decades of ghosthood have destroyed about 95 percent of the town. Yet, the Bodie that remains is a real gem. Frozen in time, Bodie's heart and soul live on in this current view stretching from the wooden Methodist church on the left to the Standard Mine's corrugated metal buildings on the upper right slope.

**ABOVE** Another view of the town from the Standard Mine.

**BELOW** Spared from fire, a few buildings still line Bodie's gap-toothed Main Street, which now plays host to growing grass and a soulful quiet where commerce once bustled and thousands trod.

But even before then, the glitter was fading. The mine had only so much gold, and when it was all extracted, Bodie languished and died. Two fires, in 1892 and 1932, left charred memories of any "excess" buildings that had remained after the people left. Since then, there has been no rebuilding and little restoration. What remains is lovingly maintained in a state of "arrested decay."

# Darwin, California

Everyone turned out in their finest for the arrival of the stage in Darwin around 1900. Even the dog sitting between the two ladies in front of the Cosmopolitan Restaurant donned a dress bandana.

The desiccated, ragtag silver-mining ghost of Darwin nestles against the bone-dry Darwin Hills, smack-dab in the middle of moonscape desert west of Death Valley. It was named after Dr. E. Darwin French, an explorer who led an 1860 prospecting trip into the desert east of the Sierras searching for the legendary Lost Gunsight lode, a supposed ledge of pure silver reportedly discovered by a California gold rush–bound argonaut.

**ABOVE** Downtown Darwin's crossroads at Main Street and Market Street is marked by a cluster of ancient businesses such as The Outpost with its canopied false front, fading paint, and dead gas pumps that once dispensed Shell gasoline to travelers. This building is said to have started life in the 1920s as a pool hall before being reborn and remodeled into a café. It later served as a general store, gas station, and post office. The current post office operates out of a more recently constructed building elsewhere in town.

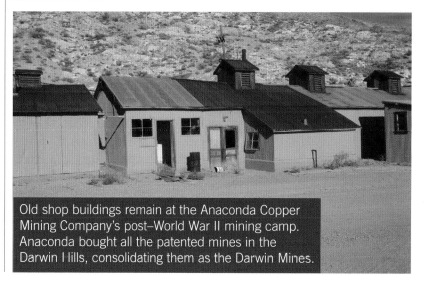

Old shop buildings remain at the Anaconda Copper Mining Company's post–World War II mining camp. Anaconda bought all the patented mines in the Darwin Hills, consolidating them as the Darwin Mines.

The traveler lost a rifle sight and, in searching for it, found a rich outcropping of silver ore, out of which he carved a new sight. A legend born—a ledge lost.

French's party was unsuccessful, but it did locate rich silver outcroppings at Coso, California, opening up the desert for additional discoveries. In 1874, silver-lead ore was found northeast of Coso, resulting in the mining camp named after Dr. French. By 1875, Darwin was a wild boomtown. Crude and rowdy, Darwin had more than 1,000 folks in 1876. Mining eventually slowed, labor disputes arose, and other boomtowns beckoned. Darwin withered quickly, its citizenry scattering. By 1880, a mere six years after the town was founded, only 85 people remained.

# Randsburg, California

In the 1970s, these three little false fronts on the south side of Butte Avenue were packed with antiques for sale. Restoration has brought new life to these old buildings.

**N**o airs here. This is the real thing, barely hanging in there by the nails on the hands of its 99 residents in the 2020 census. Founded in 1895, Randsburg is colorful, dusty, and honest, wearing its mining heritage and resultant ambiance well. Its one-time boom is long gone, as is the 100-stamp mill, the $20 million in gold, and the 1,500 to 2,500 residents who pried it from the ground.

Butte Avenue, Randsburg's main street, is lined with century-old false fronts, a curled boardwalk, and memories of the glory days so vivid they can be photographed. The general store is still open, serving the needs of the locals and tourists alike.

A couple of saloons still dispense food, drinks, and advice. And the tiny but surprisingly well-stocked museum opens its doors to the public on the weekends. Mining equipment and mine headframes decorate the town and the dry, dusty, hills that surround it.

Only missing its wooden sidewalk and batwing doors, the White House Saloon comes straight out of the Old West.

# Salton Sea, California

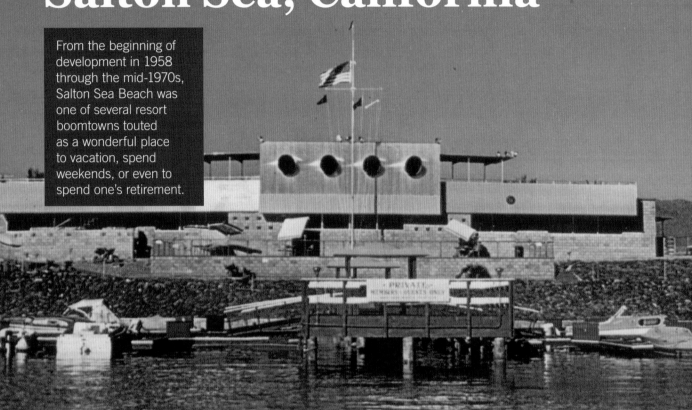

From the beginning of development in 1958 through the mid-1970s, Salton Sea Beach was one of several resort boomtowns touted as a wonderful place to vacation, spend weekends, or even to spend one's retirement.

The Salton Sea fills a sub-sea level basin almost as deep as Death Valley's famed Badwater, and it is a basin whose only outlet is through evaporation.

The sea's history is unusual, caused by a colossal "oops" in planning for irrigation in 1905. That error allowed the rampaging Colorado River to escape its normal banks and run wild off to the north into the Salton Sink. Two years later, the river's flow was returned toward the Gulf of California, but by then California had a new lake.

Minor shoreline improvement began shortly after that, but it wasn't until 1958 that major development turned the Salton Sea into California's Riviera: a bustling fishing, boating, and recreational paradise. Salton City, Salton Sea Beach, Desert Shores, North Shore, and Bombay

**ABOVE** A photo of a salt-crusted dock along a pier at the North Shore Yatch Club.

Beach thrived, drawing thousands of visitors daily for roughly the next 20 years.

Then came the summers of 1976 and 1977. Torrential rains from a pair of tropical storms transformed that Riviera into a memory. Resorts, marinas, and small communities ringing the sea were partially flooded or disappeared entirely into the increasingly saline waters, proof that even a one-foot water rise can have disastrous impacts in a flat desert basin.

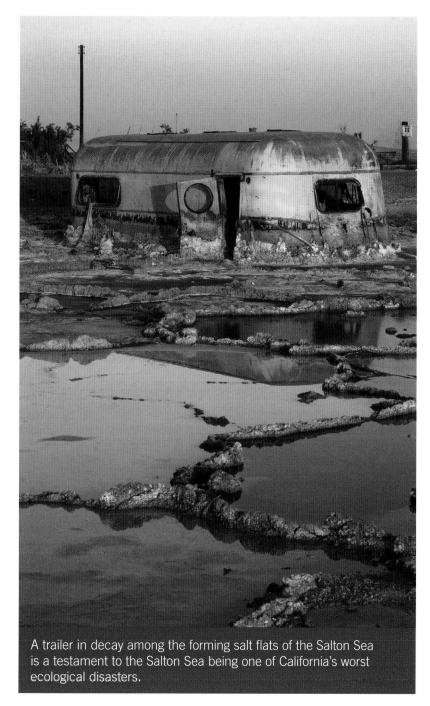

A trailer in decay among the forming salt flats of the Salton Sea is a testament to the Salton Sea being one of California's worst ecological disasters.

# Belmont, Nevada

Built in February 1868, the 40-stamp Combination Mill just east of Belmont crushed a good share of the $15 million in silver-lead ores produced in the area. In 1915, it was torn down; the bricks were reused to build the Cameron Mill. The tall smokestack on the right still stands.

In his book, *Preserving the Glory Days*, author and historian Shawn Hall calls Belmont, "The Queen of Nye County's ghost towns." And he's right. Once home to about 4,000 people, Belmont is just a shadow of the bustling silver mining town it once was. Founded in 1865, Belmont had—within a year—become the crazed focus of a major silver rush and a small city. In 1867, the town obtained the Nye County seat, a position it held until 1905, when Tonopah wrested the honor. But by then, Belmont was gasping for air.

In between, Belmont experienced 40 years of excitement. Due to the rich silver mines that pumped out more than $15 million, it lasted longer than most mining camps. Amenities of the town included boarding houses, a brewery, a church, a fire department, fraternal organizations, general stores, a livery stable, newspapers, restaurants, saloons, sawmills, a stage line, and an undertaker.

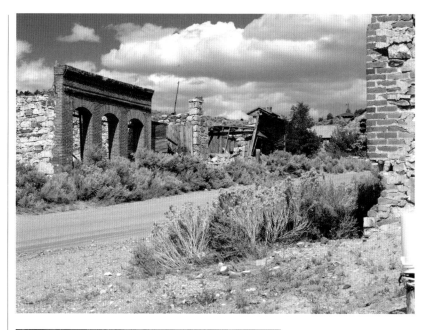

**ABOVE** Ruins and rubble mark the once-bustling heart of one of Nevada's largest silver mining towns.

**LEFT** Nearly ten years after Belmont snagged the county seat from the town of Ione, its two-story brick courthouse was open, serving the county until 1905.

In 1914, Belmont's ghosts were dusted off, and the post office and mines reopened. After an eight-year run that saw another million dollars in silver added to the total production, however, they all closed again in 1922.

Today's Belmont is considerably different from the Belmont of 1880. Newer cabins dot the hillsides, and a bed-and-breakfast and an operating saloon serve those who visit. The massive brick courthouse, ruins of three ore mills, and the cemetery compete with a crumbling Main Street for attention. Along Main Street, roofless and frontless rock buildings mix with wooden buildings reduced to piles of kindling. This magnificent relic of Americana is located about an hour's drive northeast of Tonopah.

# Grafton, Utah

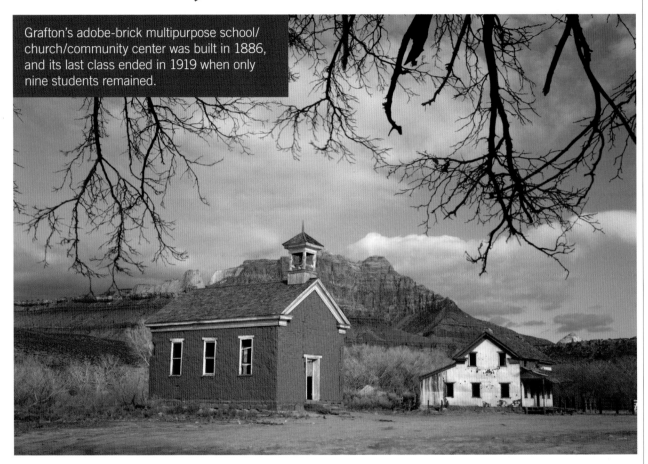

Grafton's adobe-brick multipurpose school/church/community center was built in 1886, and its last class ended in 1919 when only nine students remained.

**G**rafton was established by Mormon farmers on the south side of the Virgin River in 1859, part of the colonization process the Mormon Church undertook in Southern Utah (which they called Dixie) in the mid- and late-1800s. The Virgin is unpredictable, and in 1862 it rose against the settlers, washing away their town.

So they relocated to higher ground, set out fruit orchards, planted corn and wheat, raised sheep, dabbled in cotton, and grew mulberry trees for the production of silk. Prosperity never arrived, however, and because of disease and Native American incursions, the town was abandoned for a

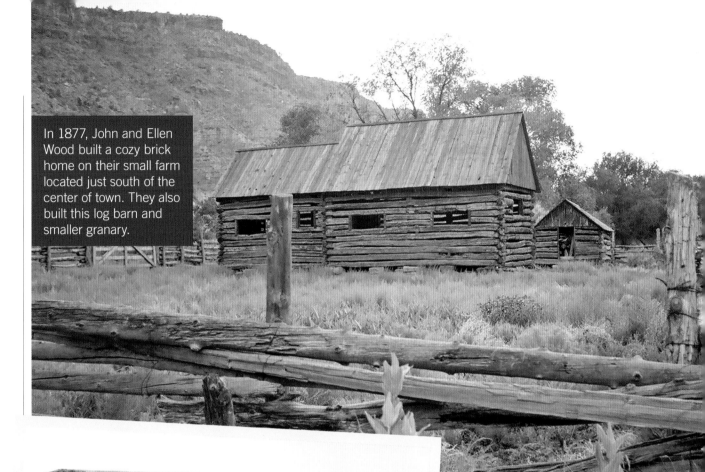

In 1877, John and Ellen Wood built a cozy brick home on their small farm located just south of the center of town. They also built this log barn and smaller granary.

**ABOVE** Located on a raised area a half-mile south of the town site, Grafton's cemetery holds graves dated from 1862 to 1924. Many are unmarked, but others tell stories of hardship, death, and much grieving among these sturdy pioneers trying to eke out a home in the wilderness, truly strangers in an unfriendly land.

short time between 1866 and 1868.

The peak population of Grafton appears to have been less than 200, and by 1920 only three families remained. The site has been used for the filming of several movies, including parts of *Butch Cassidy and the Sundance Kid*.

# The Tintic, Utah

Sitting in a draw midway up the north side of Eureka Ridge, south of Eureka itself, the Centennial-Eureka Mine was one of the largest mines in the Tintic Mining District. This image dates to around 1900 when the mine employed about 100 workers. It closed in 1927 after producing around 45,000 ounces of gold and 21 million ounces of silver.

Silver, silver, silver! That's what the Tintic Mining District was all about, more than $50 million in silver. The name came from Ute Chief Tintic, a name which the capitalists gladly disgraced. This historic silver mining district straddles U.S. Highway 6, about 25 miles west of Interstate 15 at Santaquin. Today, the Tintic is a collection of forgotten names such as Dividend, Homansville, and Knightsville; rubbled sites such as Silver City; sleepy places such as Mammoth; and the area's metropolis: Eureka, with its nearly 700 residents and a very ghostly air.

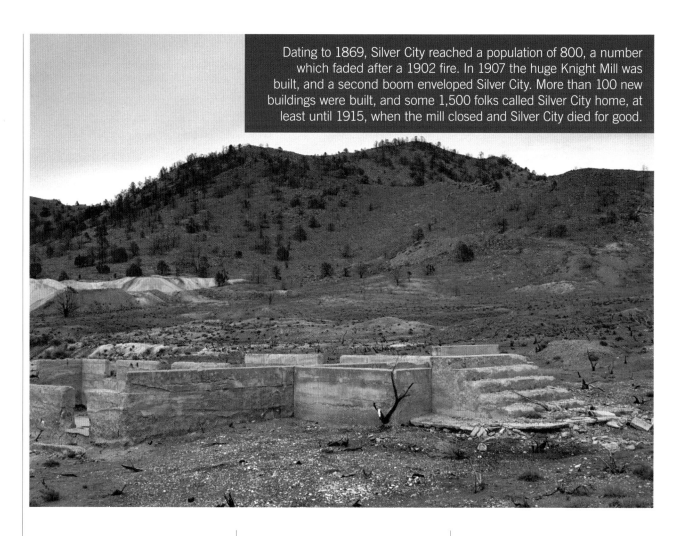

Dating to 1869, Silver City reached a population of 800, a number which faded after a 1902 fire. In 1907 the huge Knight Mill was built, and a second boom enveloped Silver City. More than 100 new buildings were built, and some 1,500 folks called Silver City home, at least until 1915, when the mill closed and Silver City died for good.

Eureka's long main street is lined with mostly unoccupied buildings, all of which harken back to when it was the boom town of the Tintic. Silver was discovered here in December 1869; after subsequent discoveries, the true value of the deposits was realized, and Eureka quickly placed itself at the leading edge of the district. Fire ravaged Eureka in 1893, but the town quickly rebuilt with one- and two-story brick and stone buildings, most of which remain intact today.

In 1910, Eureka had a population of 3,400 as well as the second J. C. Penney store in the country. In 1930, Eureka still had 3,041 folks, and it wasn't until 1942, when the mines were closed by Order L-208, that Eureka's population declined radically.

South of Eureka is the old town of Mammoth, where a fire station, cabins, and lots of rubble remain. The mine sits above the town on the side of a hill. In 1930, 750 people still lived in Mammoth, but only a few are there now.

On April 21, 1906, teachers from Juab and Eureka gathered for a convention at the four-year-old Church of Jesus Christ of Latter Day Saints meeting house. It was one of several churches in Eureka, and its Gothic Revival style stands out among the others.

**RIGHT** Dead buildings, boarded-up windows, faded advertisements, peeling paint, cracked concrete sidewalks, and crumbling storefronts mark Eureka's Main Street today. The historic value of this now-quiet town and surrounding mining district was recognized in 1979 when Eureka and the Tintic Mining District were listed with the National Register of Historic Places.

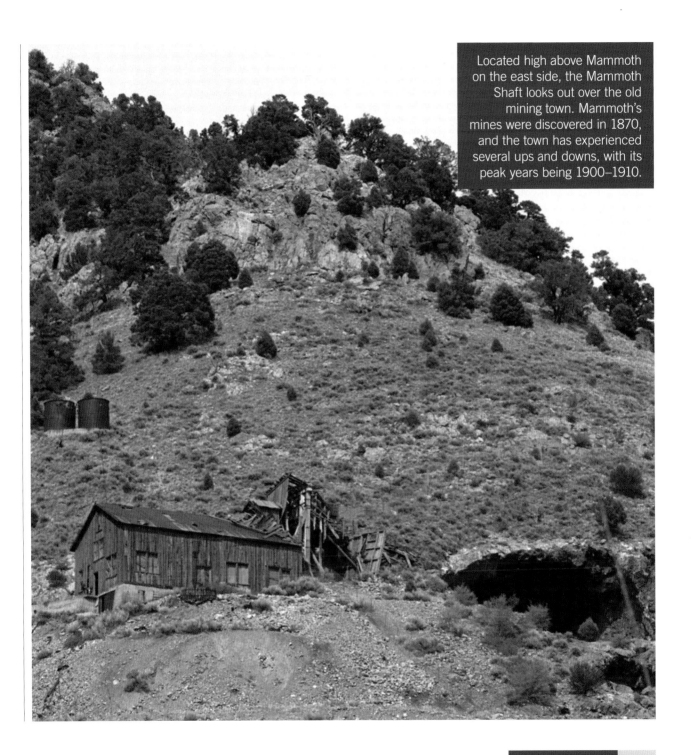

Located high above Mammoth on the east side, the Mammoth Shaft looks out over the old mining town. Mammoth's mines were discovered in 1870, and the town has experienced several ups and downs, with its peak years being 1900–1910.

# Topaz, Utah

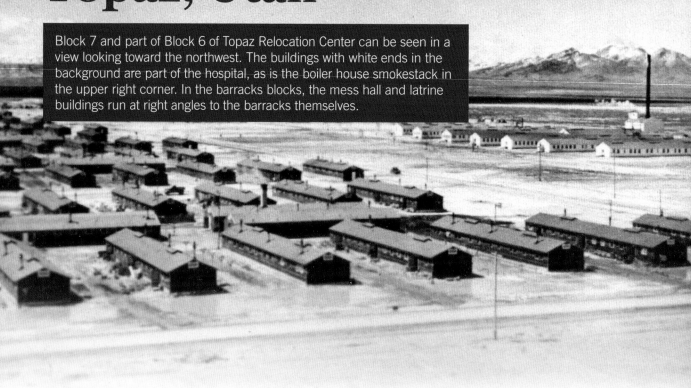

Block 7 and part of Block 6 of Topaz Relocation Center can be seen in a view looking toward the northwest. The buildings with white ends in the background are part of the hospital, as is the boiler house smokestack in the upper right corner. In the barracks blocks, the mess hall and latrine buildings run at right angles to the barracks themselves.

Shortly after the fateful morning of December 7, 1941, when the Japanese Navy attacked Pearl Harbor, the United States of America was swept up in a wave of anti-Japanese hysteria. It didn't take long into 1942 before ten relocation centers scattered about the American West were hastily banged together to hold Japanese Americans. Consisting of 623 buildings, Topaz Relocation Center was built in the western Utah desert about 16 miles northwest of Delta. Opening on September 11, 1942, it became the new home for more than 8,000 detainees, which made it Utah's fifth largest city. The entire complex covered 19,800 acres, but the main portion was a square-mile core of buildings in 42 numbered blocks.

When World War II ended, these camps were no longer needed, so on October 31,

1945, Topaz was closed. The buildings were removed shortly thereafter.

As a plaque at the entrance of the main site reads: "The memory of Topaz remains a tribute to a people whose faith and loyalty was steadfast—while America's had faltered."

**ABOVE** This photograph circa 1942 shows relocated Japanese American internees unloading their belongings and moving into the barracks at the Central Utah Relocation Center, later renamed Topaz Relocation Center. Most of the detainees at this camp were from the San Francisco Bay area.

# Animas Forks, Colorado

In this photograph circa 1878, Animas Forks was a small town of 30 homes and 250 people, a general store, a post office, and a saloon. By 1885 it had doubled in population to 450 people, and its businesses consisted of two assay offices, a boarding house, a hotel, and several saloons and stores.

Sitting at an elevation of 11,184 feet in the mine-studded Animas River Valley in the heart of the San Juan Mountains of southwest Colorado, Animas Forks is one of the highest ghost towns in the country, and 450 people called this valley home—at least in the summer—until the 1890s, when it began to fade.

Still standing is the famous two-story William Duncan House, with its magnificent bay windows, that unfounded local legend says was once owned by Tom Walsh, the owner of the nearby Camp Bird Mine above Ouray. He sold his mine holdings in 1902 to

**ABOVE** Looking almost like a watercolor painting, the Frisco-Bagley Mine, its 150-ton electrical-powered reduction mill, and the mine manager's house decorate the slope above the West Fork of the Animas River, a half mile west of Animas Forks.

**RIGHT** The scattered remnants of Animas Forks, such as the two-story William Duncan House built in 1879, have been stabilized by the Bureau of Land Management. That was made possible by the solid construction of most of these buildings, which was necessary because of the heavy snow and long, brutal winters.

become a multimillionaire, and the family moved to Washington, D.C., where he built the famous Walsh-McLean House (which is now the Indonesian Embassy). His daughter, Evalyn Walsh, married publishing heir Edward "Ned" Beale McLean in 1908. In 1932, she inherited her parents' estate, including the mansion, when her mother died. Four years later, she wrote her memoirs, *Father Struck It Rich*. Rumor had it that she lived in the Animas Forks house while writing it. Evalyn Walsh McLean was wealthy and eccentric. She was also a socialite who, from 1911 until 1947, was the last private owner of the magnificent, deep blue, 45.52 carat Hope Diamond and its associated curse.

# Nevadaville, Colorado

**P**oor Nevadaville, sitting forgotten like a castoff light bulb. Located a mile southwest of Central City and Black Hawk, two neon-lit Rocky Mountain gambling havens, it was a key player in establishing "The Richest Square Mile on Earth." Unlike those other two towns, however, Nevadaville is quiet, sprinkled with red-brick buildings lining a dirt main street. Its ghost town aura virtually glows.

Established 1859 as Nevada City, it had 2,705 people in 1860 but was wiped off the map by a fast-moving

This view of Nevadaville looks northeast across the west end of the town. The large buildings in the foreground house the Gold Coin Mines Company Mine and Mill, and mine-studded Nevada Hill rises directly behind town in the background. Downtown Nevadaville is on the far right.

**RIGHT** Rock wall ruins are all that are left of an old store building basement on the south side of Main Street.

fire in 1861. The town bounced back, bigger and better, officially as Bald Mountain—its unpopular post office name. Nevada City/Bald Mountain peaked in the 1860s when the town blended into Central City, which in turn became part of Black Hawk, all amalgamated and mixed together like modern, faceless suburbia.

In 1868, however, there came a big compromise in which the town officially became Nevadaville. (The post office, however, remained Bald Mountain until it closed in 1921.) That wasn't enough to sustain the town, however, and Nevadaville's radiance dimmed until only two residents remained in 1930.

The two-story, brick Masonic Hall was built in 1879 to replace a building the Masons were leasing. The lodge's membership followed the town's population, and by the 1940s, the remaining members of Lodge #4 met in Central City. Lodge meetings in the 1950s featured debates on whether to sell, renovate, or tear down this building.

# St. Elmo, Colorado

The once-bustling Main Street of St. Elmo is quiet now. Visitors no longer venture in and out of Stark's Home Comfort Hotel, nor do the doors to the Stark Brothers' Store and post office open and close with the passing of shoppers. The Starks were the last of the old-time families in St. Elmo, with the final family member leaving in 1958, six years after the post office closed.

The town of St. Elmo had it all. Established around 1880 as Forest City, this booming gold town, stagecoach hub, and railroad construction camp had 400 or so people. The narrow-gauge Denver, South Park, and Pacific Railroad was punching its 1,845-foot-long Alpine Tunnel through the mountains west of St. Elmo while the mines released their treasure. But the U.S. Post Office didn't like the name Forest City. Three people got together

**ABOVE** This view looks north across the west end of Main Street from Hancock Road—which followed the Denver, South Park, and Pacific Railroad line uphill towards Romley. The large building in the center is the Stark Brothers store, the post office, and Home Comfort Hotel.

to brainstorm. Some one remembered a popular novel by Augusta Jane Evans called *St. Elmo*, and everyone agreed. Forest City was renamed St. Elmo.

Through the 1880s, St. Elmo bustled, with as many as 2,000 residents. That all changed in 1890 when fire swept through. The storekeeper/postmaster was the hero of the day, saving the mail. He couldn't save his store, however, and lost the town's cigar and liquor supply. In all, two blocks of businesses were incinerated and not rebuilt.

People moved on after that, and in 1910, the Alpine Tunnel closed, leaving St. Elmo as the end of the line. The Mary Murphy Mine kept 100 employed until 1922, when it shut down after producing 220,000 ounces of gold. Four years

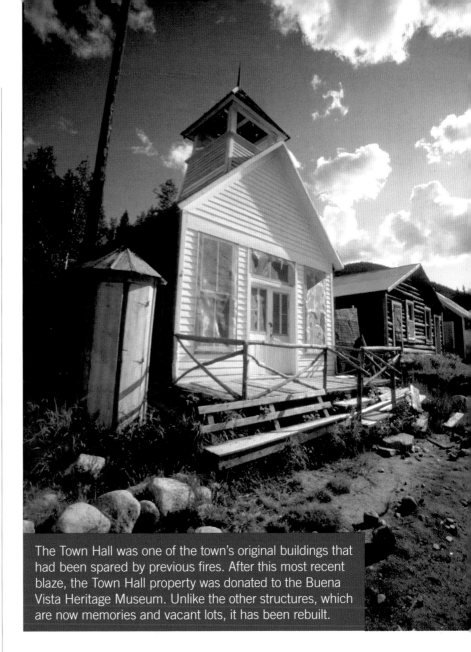

The Town Hall was one of the town's original buildings that had been spared by previous fires. After this most recent blaze, the Town Hall property was donated to the Buena Vista Heritage Museum. Unlike the other structures, which are now memories and vacant lots, it has been rebuilt.

later, the train stopped running altogether. St. Elmo looks like a ghost town should. Its 40 or so worn, wooden buildings turn empty faces onto a dirt main street in the forested Chalk River Valley uphill from Nathrop.

# Silverton, Colorado

By 1940, the date of this photo, the Silver Lake Mill, a massive, low-grade silver mining complex near Silverton, was starting to show the effects of aging and neglect. Active from 1890 to 1900, the mill burned in 1907 and was rebuilt. In its lifetime, it processed more than 500,000 tons of low-grade ore worth more than $7 million.

**S**itting in the heart of Southwestern Colorado's San Juan Mountains, Silverton was the ultimate boomtown, the Silver Queen of Colorado. Gold and silver were found by the ton in the mountains surrounding the 9,300-foot high mountain bowl along the Animas River.

Beginning in 1874, miners flocked here in droves, followed by other camp hangers-on. The town site was laid out, and within a few months the population passed the 500 mark. In 1882, the railroad arrived, and the real boom began.

**ABOVE** A row of historic buildings on the west side of Greene Street looking north toward the county courthouse, whose dome you can see peeking from the top of the last building on the right.

**LEFT** Construction began on the San Juan County courthouse in August 1906, and 16 months later it was open for business. San Juan County is the least populated of Colorado's counties, and Silverton is the only town in San Juan County.

The town turned into a city, and the population arched upward toward 3,000. Blocks of substantial buildings were erected and remain today. Fraternal lodges, churches, a library, a courthouse, and other amenities tamed the wild edge—a bit.

Silverton stumbled a little in the 1893 Silver Panic, but the first half of the 20th century was brutal to the Silver Queen. In October 1918, a flu epidemic killed 146 people. Silver lost 50 percent of its value in 1920, shuttering mines. That trend continued through 1942, when Order L-208 took care of the rest.

# Bisbee, Arizona

**B**oom and bust, copper and rust, Bisbee and its colorful assortment of 6,000 people does not meet normally accepted connotations of what a ghost town is. But behind that first impression is the truth. Bisbee has waned. Its zenith was in the early 1900s when it had around 20,000 residents.

The dry Arizona desert puckers up into mineral-rich mountains in numerous places. Just 20 miles south of Tombstone and seven miles north of the Mexico-U.S. border, the Mule Mountains are one of those puckers.

Sprawling up the arms of a V-shape gulch on the south side of the Mule Mountains is the majestic old copper-mining city of Bisbee. The Queen Mine lies below, a massive hole in the earth that yielded eight billion pounds of copper, as well as millions of ounces of gold and silver and millions of pounds of lead, zinc, and other minerals. This mine made Bisbee the undisputed "Queen of the Copper Camps" and put it on the map, keeping it there for more than 100 years.

Today's Bisbee is a funky, fun town filled with free spirits, frivolity, and festivals, all playing up the good old days. Bisbee's charm lies in the fact that a major fire completely wiped out the rambling tinderbox town in 1908. By 1910, however, the ashes were replaced by what is there now, a living museum filled with 1910 architecture.

The Lavender Pit, viewed here from the north, was Bisbee's true "Money Pit" until December 1974. This money pit didn't absorb money, however; it produced massive quantities of it.

# Goldroad and Oatman, Arizona

In 1900, Jose Jerez discovered gold west of Sitgreaves Pass, and in 1902, Ben Paddock (some sources say Taddock) found gold at the Elephant's Tooth, a monolith at today's Oatman. Both discoverers sold out to organized mining companies that quickly moved in. *Kaching*! At Goldroad, the little gold camp played sweet music off and on, ran a population of several hundred, and finally shut down in 1942. In 1949 the buildings were semidismantled so the owner wouldn't have to pay property taxes on usable but empty buildings.

Oatman's story differs, however. The Vivian post office opened in 1904 then

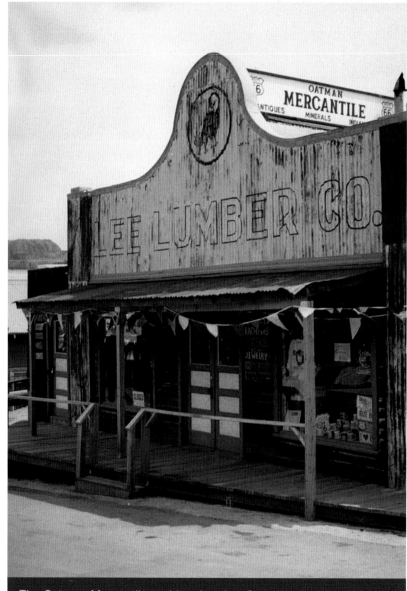

The Oatman Mercantile and Lee Lumber Company building is one of many ancient, weathered, and repainted storefronts along Main Street catering to the 500,000 tourists who flock annually to see a tiny part of the Old West and Route 66.

**ABOVE** The 300-seat former Oatman Theatre Building stopped showing movies by 1945. Here it is housing a retail store, and its shady porch provides a great place to sit and watch life, and the ubiquitous burros, march up and down the street.

changed names to Oatman in 1909. Oatman's mines were richer, and the location was better than Goldroad. Wild, younger brother Oatman quickly outgrew and outperformed its civic sibling. Some 10,000 people flocked here, but they left just as quickly when the Tom Reed Mine shut down in the 1930s. That left Oatman's remaining folks to cater to travelers along Route 66, which lasted until the 1950s, when the road was realigned, isolating Oatman and its 60 residents.

**LEFT** The Goldroad Mine kept the town of Goldroad alive until the operation closed in 1942. New owners reopened the mine in 1995, producing gold until 1998, when it shut down again. Tours of the underground workings were offered until 2007.

# Superior, Arizona

**W**elcome to Superior, Arizona. Like Bisbee, Arizona; Silverton, Colorado; and Galena, Illinois, Superior is a living town, a byproduct from the flush days of when it was a booming copper mining outpost. It still has a large resident population. But Superior has a unique twist: The main business district is dead—not just a few scattered buildings, but a solidly lined, dead main street.

Superior has seen little print in ghost-town literature, but it is a true gem dating to 1910 when the Magma Copper Mining Company purchased the former Silver King mine and support town of Superior (renamed from Hastings in 1900). Magma went for the copper and found it. With more than 4,000 people during

Perched at the far eastern end of Main Street, the La Mina Bar on the left side of the block is one of a few businesses still operating in downtown Superior. Just to its right, Griffen's Market runs a perpetual "SALE" in a vacant building.

the Great Depression, Superior was one of the few bright economic spots in a depressed economy.

But its prosperity is fading. In 1970, the census recorded 5,028 folks, but the July 2020 Census Bureau estimate was down to 2,407. Superior's copper mines are now quiet. The dead downtown beckons. The ghosts are encroaching.

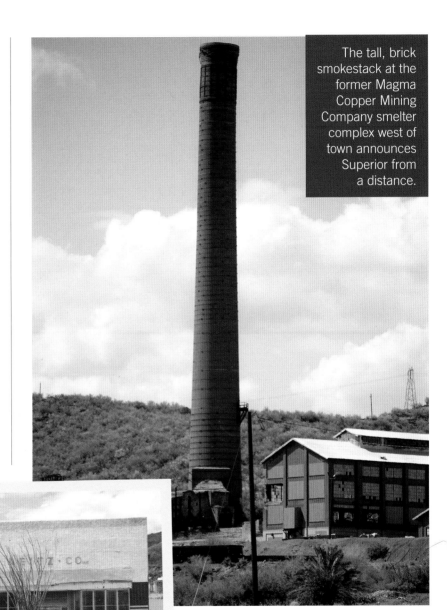

The tall, brick smokestack at the former Magma Copper Mining Company smelter complex west of town announces Superior from a distance.

**LEFT** Scattered throughout many of Arizona's dead and dying mining towns are the bright red-and-white shells of Sprouse Reitz Company's five & dime stores. Many, however, were sited in early- to mid–20th-century mining towns.

# Vulture Mine, Arizona

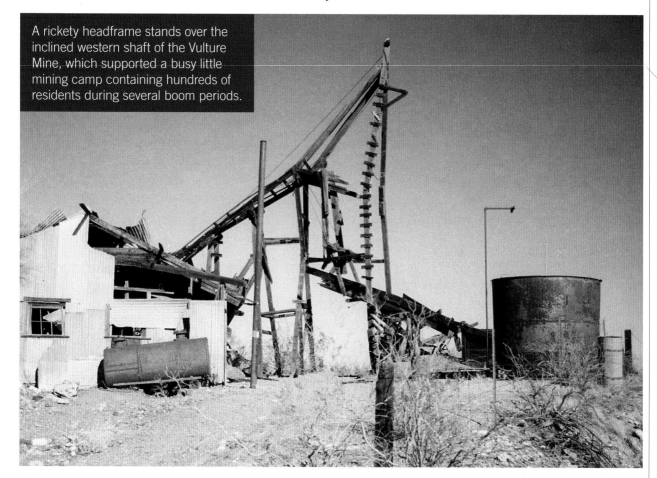

A rickety headframe stands over the inclined western shaft of the Vulture Mine, which supported a busy little mining camp containing hundreds of residents during several boom periods.

**H**enry Wickenburg was a real character. How did he come to find and name the rich gold ledge that evolved into the Vulture Mine? The year was 1863 and Wickenburg was out prospecting and saw a group of vultures soaring around what is now Vulture Peak. Or, so the story goes, Wickenburg saw the vultures and shot one. When he went to pick it up, he came across a number of gold nuggets lying around where the bird fell.

Believe it or not, that is just one of many fabulous stories of the Vulture Mine's origin. Wickenburg established his mine and then leased it out. In 1866, he sold an 80-percent interest in it to some New Yorkers—he only received the $20,000 down payment out of the total $85,000 promised, however.

Even after litigation, he never got the balance, nor any returns on his one-fifth share. Bitter and broken, Wickenburg retired to his ranch outside the nearby town of Wickenburg, where in 1905 he shot himself in the head, ending his long, often painful, life. The Vulture Mine possibly produced as much as $200 million in gold.

**RIGHT** This crumbling adobe is said to have been a hotel, but legend maintains that the "hotel" housed single ladies rather than travelers. It opened in the 1870s and closed in 1942, when the entire camp shut down for the duration of World War II.

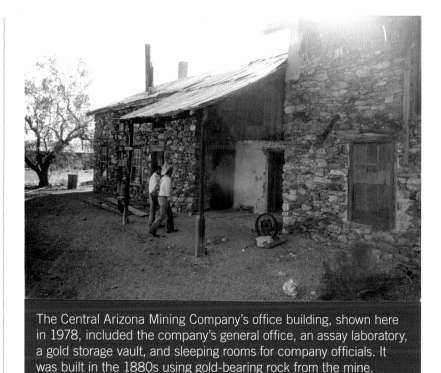

The Central Arizona Mining Company's office building, shown here in 1978, included the company's general office, an assay laboratory, a gold storage vault, and sleeping rooms for company officials. It was built in the 1880s using gold-bearing rock from the mine.

# Chloride, New Mexico

Of the 30 or so remaining buildings in Chloride, these two are the best known. The restored Monte Cristo saloon graces the left, and the Pioneer Store Museum is on the right. Both are listed on the State Register of Cultural Properties.

English teamster Harry Pye's claim to fame was that he found a rich silver lead in 1879 and was supposedly killed by Apache a few months later while working his claims. His legacy: Chloride, New Mexico.

Chloride was established in 1880, its tents filling the canyon bottom along Chloride Creek at the mouth of Chloride Creek Canyon in the Black Range mountains northwest of Truth or Consequences. In 1881, a real townsite was laid out, and seven businesses and 20 houses were built. Chloride boomed through the 1880s and began to decline after the silver market crashed in 1893. Even though Chloride faded, however, it was never totally abandoned. As a

**ABOVE** Chloride is filled with many different buildings of various designs and materials. This steep-roofed rock home was built in 1921 by longtime resident Austin Crawford. In July 1997, the house was added to New Mexico Historic Preservation Division's State Register of Cultural Properties.

**BELOW** Located nine miles west of Chloride, the Silver Monument Mine was the largest and most productive of the mines that supported the town. Through 1926, it produced $680,000 in silver.

result, a number of old buildings remain along with 20 or so residents.

In 1977, the fate of Chloride was changed by a retired couple. Don and Dona Edmund were touring the back roads of New Mexico looking for unique and interesting places to visit and possibly settle. Upon arriving in Chloride, they knew this was to be their new home. They purchased a house and settled down amidst the handful of remaining old-timers, the last of whom passed away in 1999. Over time the Edmunds purchased more property and buildings, restoring many, including the 1880 Pioneer Store building built by James Dalglish. That location is now operated as the Pioneer Store Museum.

# Lake Valley, New Mexico

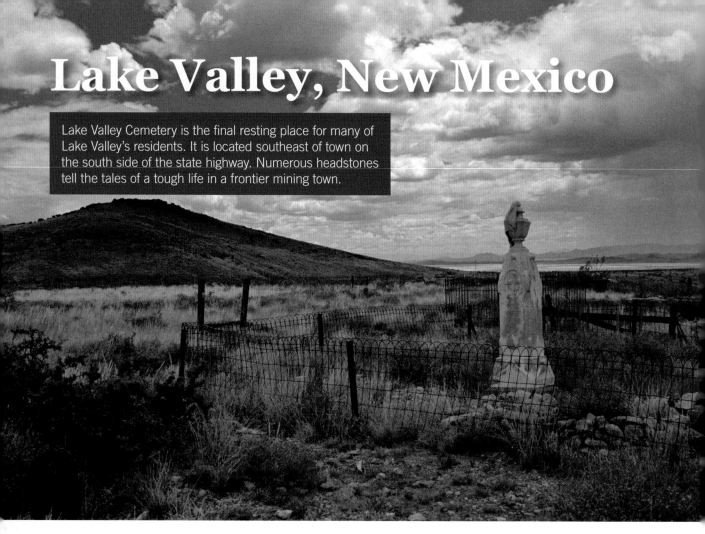

Lake Valley Cemetery is the final resting place for many of Lake Valley's residents. It is located southeast of town on the south side of the state highway. Numerous headstones tell the tales of a tough life in a frontier mining town.

Lake Valley's boom-bust cycles began with the discovery of rich silver ore by George Lufkin in August 1878. Other claims were staked, and development began. George Daly, a mining promoter, arrived and purchased all those claims.

Deep in one of these mines, a massive ore pocket of almost pure silver was discovered—silver crystals glittered in the light from miner's candles. Called the Bridal Chamber, its value surpassed $15,000 per ton. Needless to say, Lake Valley boomed, quickly sprawling into a rowdy mining town supporting more than a thousand residents.

In 1893, the national silver panic crippled mining, and Lake Valley quickly faded. A major fire in June 1895 decimated the town, leaving little for the couple hundred residents still there. What remained barely clung to life through the first half of the 20th century.

The railroad shut down in 1934. Some manganese was mined in the mid-1940s and 1950s, but the post office finally closed in 1954, along with the mine and the rest of town. Lake Valley's last residents hung in there until 1994, when the Bureau of Land Management arrived.

**BELOW** Photographer Henry Schmidt photographed his own house in Lake Valley on July 4, 1897. Schmidt was a well-known assayer and photographer in the region, taking many pictures of the buildings and mines in the mining towns of Lake Valley, Chloride, Winston, and Tyrone.

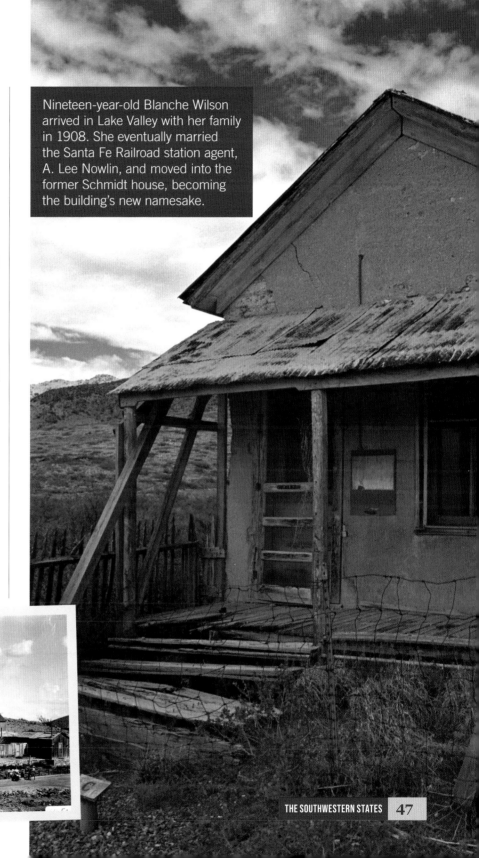

Nineteen-year-old Blanche Wilson arrived in Lake Valley with her family in 1908. She eventually married the Santa Fe Railroad station agent, A. Lee Nowlin, and moved into the former Schmidt house, becoming the building's new namesake.

# Mogollon, New Mexico

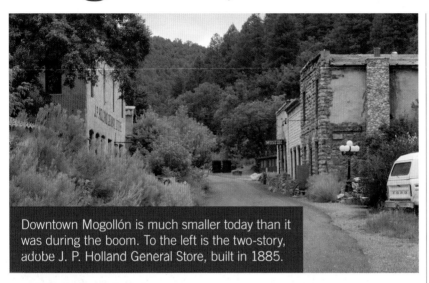

Downtown Mogollón is much smaller today than it was during the boom. To the left is the two-story, adobe J. P. Holland General Store, built in 1885.

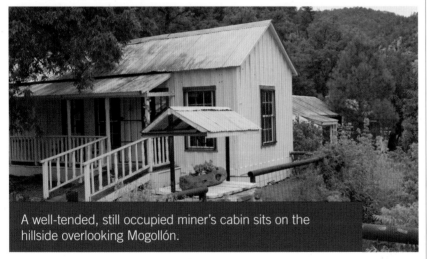

A well-tended, still occupied miner's cabin sits on the hillside overlooking Mogollón.

Mogollón (pronounced mo-gee-YON) also seemed to suffer from a Sodom and Gomorrah complex, enduring the scourges of fire five times (in 1894, 1904, 1910, 1915, and 1942) and flood four times (in 1894, 1896, 1899, and 1914). Because of its isolation, this 20th-century mining town was steeped in 19th-century mining town morals. In fact, prohibition during the 1920s was pretty much ignored.

That might just sum up Mogollón, one of the state's best ghost towns. Despite being continuously burned out and washed out, as well as being ignored by the outside world—as long as its mineral wealth continued to flow—it boomed and busted several times en route to its final destiny in 1942 with Order L-208 and a final major fire.

In this wild mining town of 2,000 people, a reputed 14 saloons, and a pair of red-light districts, it seemed $20 million in gold and silver taken from the ground may been secondary to liquor, women, gunplay, and robbery.

The Little Fannie Mine is on the site of the original silver/gold discovery in the 1870s, but it wasn't until the 1880s that any serious work occurred.

# Route 66 Ghost Towns in Texas

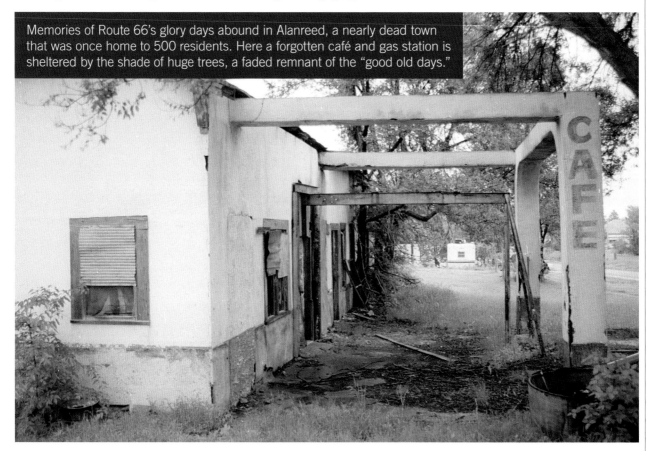

Memories of Route 66's glory days abound in Alanreed, a nearly dead town that was once home to 500 residents. Here a forgotten café and gas station is sheltered by the shade of huge trees, a faded remnant of the "good old days."

**R**oute 66 was America's Main Street, the Mother Road, the westward route of the Okies during the Dust Bowl days. Stretching from Chicago to Santa Monica, California, it stitches together eight states. In Texas, Route 66 zipped across 178 miles of griddle-flat panhandle stretching east and west of Amarillo. Only 9 percent of that pioneering route in Texas is lost; the rest is still drivable but has mostly been supplanted by Interstate 40. And in the Panhandle, ghosts of the old road towns remain, ripe for exploring.

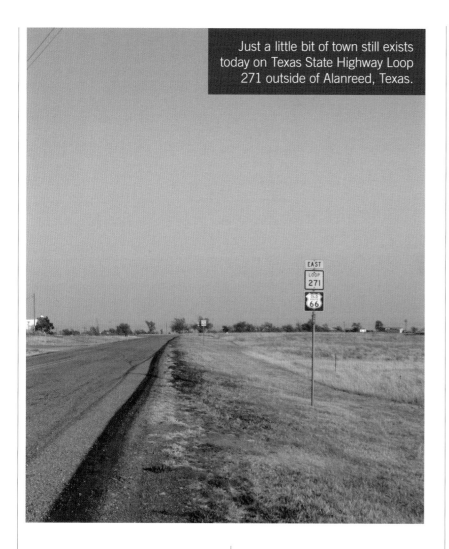

Just a little bit of town still exists today on Texas State Highway Loop 271 outside of Alanreed, Texas.

With modern air-conditioned supercars cruising effortlessly down superwide superhighways, it's hard to imagine the difficulties encountered driving this route in its heyday from the 1930s to the '60s. Unlike today, drivers couldn't cruise for 300 or 400 miles without stopping. As a result, tiny towns popped up along the highway to serve the needs of travelers as well as to entertain them, protect them from the brutal heat and blowing dust in the summer, and keep them warm and cozy in the vicious cold of winter.

Today's forgotten map dots were yesterday's road towns. Glenrio, Alanreed, and a handful of other places provided comfort and service to travelers unsticking themselves from front seats and kids crawling stiffly out of back seats. Warm "eats," hot coffee, a tank of gas—"check under the hood?"—Minuteman service, and the U-Drop-Inn with its refrigerated air and free TV. All this was provided with a smile, all designed to make the traveler feel human again. This wasn't just America's Main Street. This was America.

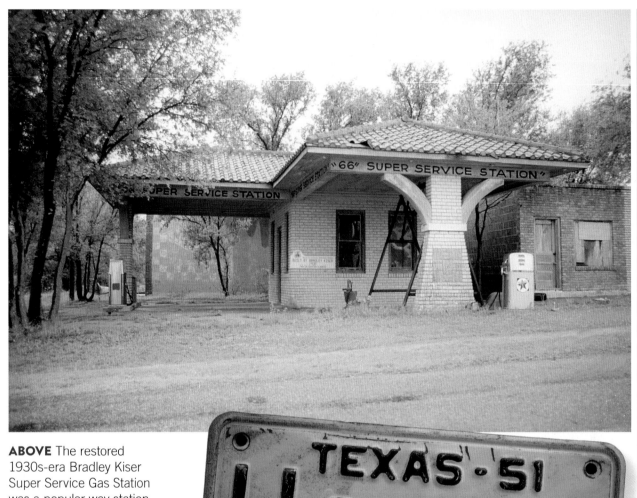

**ABOVE** The restored 1930s-era Bradley Kiser Super Service Gas Station was a popular way station in the tiny community of Alanreed. Today Alanreed barely clings to life as I-40 skirts along the north edge of town bringing some nostalgia-seeking tourists.

**RIGHT** This 1951 Texas license plate is a relic of the glory years of the little road towns scattered across the top of Texas along Route 66.

The desiccated road town of Glenrio is split by the New Mexico/Texas state line nearly dead center between the east and west anchors of Route 66. Depending on the direction of travel, it was either the first or last stop in Texas.

# Thurber, Texas

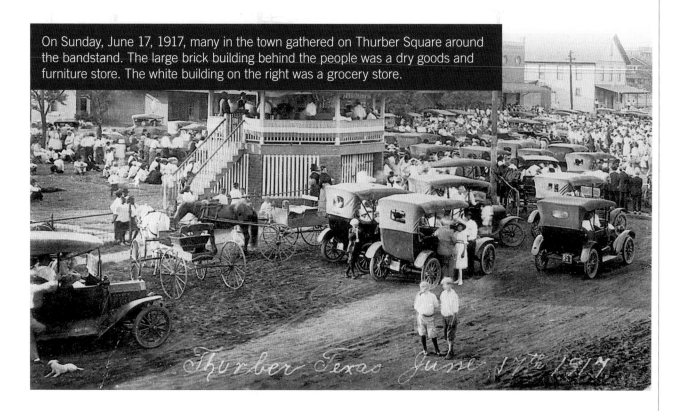

On Sunday, June 17, 1917, many in the town gathered on Thurber Square around the bandstand. The large brick building behind the people was a dry goods and furniture store. The white building on the right was a grocery store.

**A**t Thurber's mid-1910s peak, some 3,000 tons of coal a day poured from the Texas and Pacific Coal Company, union-operated underground mines dug by miners from nearly 20 nations. In 1917, oil was discovered nearby, and Thurber expanded to accommodate that industry. However, oil also contributed to the town's downfall, as the main market for coal was the railroads, which were converting locomotives over to oil burners, reducing the need for coal. Oil became popular and displaced coal, but the oil industry isn't as labor intensive and doesn't require the same numbers of workers.

In 1921, with coal production decreasing, the company proposed a devastating 33-percent wage reduction. The union countered with a 20-percent offer, which

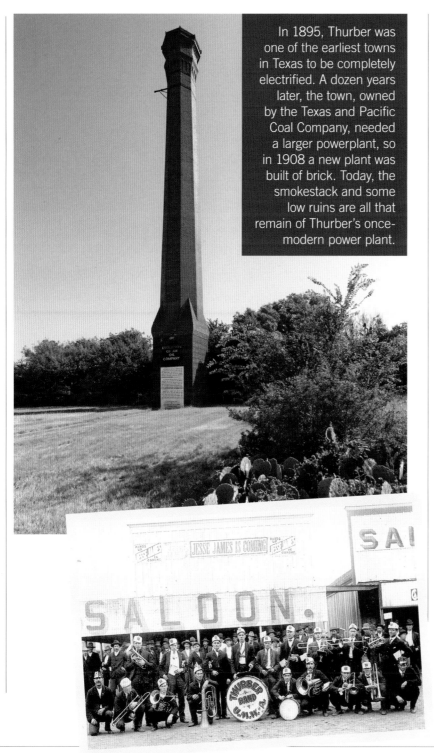

In 1895, Thurber was one of the earliest towns in Texas to be completely electrified. A dozen years later, the town, owned by the Texas and Pacific Coal Company, needed a larger powerplant, so in 1908 a new plant was built of brick. Today, the smokestack and some low ruins are all that remain of Thurber's once-modern power plant.

the company rejected. The mines were shut down, and a decade later, the brick kiln closed. Thurber's reason to exist was gone. By the end of the 1930s, the post office had closed, the last inhabitants had left, and most of the structures had been torn down. Thurber said goodbye.

Today, only mine-scarred hills, ruins, and half a dozen seen-better-days brick structures remain, including the famous 128-foot-tall smokestack, the old store (which is now a restaurant), and a museum.

**LEFT** One of Thurber's several bands was comprised of members of the United Mine Workers of America, Local Union 2763. Note the union's identification on the drum head, reflecting the fact that Thurber's mines were 100-percent unionized by 1903.

# THE NORTHWESTERN STATES

Time has been unkind to these weather-battered, wooden buildings sandwiching a habitable home in Elkhorn, Montana.

**This is the landscape traversed from 1803 to 1806 by Lewis and Clark's Corps of Discovery and 42 years later by the Oregon Trail. Beaver hunters, mountain men, and gold miners opened the country. Log forts along the seacoast, silver mining camps perched on high rocky cliffs in the interior mountains, and lonely railroad boomtowns on Wyoming's High Plains all anchored settlement, leaving thousands of unique and interesting places to explore.**

## An Influx of Settlers

Settlement of the Northwest was slow. After Lewis and Clark, the first wave of explorers washed over the region from approximately 1810 until 1840. These fur trappers and traders spread across the region in search of beaver. In 1841, however, with the rapid demise of demand for beaver pelts, they dispersed, leaving the area to new settlers drawn to Oregon's rich-soiled Willamette Valley. Stretching from present-day Eugene north to Portland, this valley was the focus of an 1840s land rush to Oregon and the final destination for more than 50,000 settlers who braved the four- to six-month, 2,000-mile journey from the area around Independence, Missouri.

During this time, the territory was jointly controlled by the United States and Britain, but in 1846, the region came completely under U.S. jurisdiction. In 1848, the discovery of gold in California created a sudden

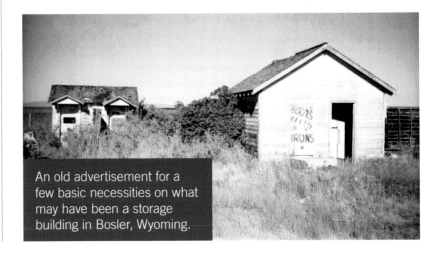

An old advertisement for a few basic necessities on what may have been a storage building in Bosler, Wyoming.

national interest in gold mining. Some 200,000 travelers trekked west across the Oregon Trail, with many turning south into the California gold fields. A string of military posts were established within eyeshot of the road to help protect and sell provisions to travelers.

**BELOW** Abandoned and alone, this ghostly real estate office building in Molson, Washington, is being reclaimed from the lush greenery nurtured by the abundant rain and snow of the Northwest.

By the early 1850s, the initial excitement of the Gold Rush had worn off, and a strong interest in prospecting for precious metals across the Northwest created periodic ripples of interest when rich lodes of gold or silver were discovered. Unlike the Southwest, however, there was no discernible pattern to the rushes.

## A Diversity of Livelihoods

Once the mining booms settled down, folks focused on the richness of the region's soil and water. The banks of the lower Columbia River were lined with small fishing villages, and canneries popped up along with supporting camps and towns. Stretching east of the Cascade Mountains into the far eastern plains, agriculture took hold. Farming and cattle towns were established, most flourishing through the middle of the 1900s. Gold and silver mining spread east into the upper Rockies and other mountain ranges in Idaho, Wyoming, and western Montana.

In the late 1800s, the grassy plains of Montana and Wyoming supported large ranches. Logging spread rapidly throughout the forested regions, where ephemeral logging camps sprouted like weeds in a tilled field. With all these new points of civilization popping up all over, the need for coal, transportation, and other commodities increased. Railroad lines pushed across the landscape, bringing construction camps, stations, railroad repair facilities, and towns to support those activities. Fuel was needed for the trains, so coal mining became big business, especially in southern Wyoming and the hills south of Seattle. Military posts remained, but many, such as Fort Laramie, Wyoming, for example, began to serve the civilian traveler population. These former forts became bustling trading posts and travel supply centers, a far cry from their original intent of providing military defense and offense.

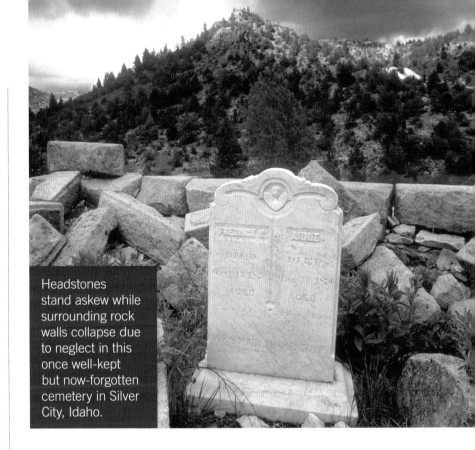

Headstones stand askew while surrounding rock walls collapse due to neglect in this once well-kept but now-forgotten cemetery in Silver City, Idaho.

## A Changing Region

As the 20th century reached its midpoint, the need for the high number of tiny towns began to fade, especially in the agricultural realm. Chesterfield, Idaho, and Jay Em, Wyoming, are two good examples of these dead agricultural communities. Mechanization of farming, long-distance vehicles that allowed more freedom of movement, and the switching of trains from coal to diesel power all caused a demise in the need for so many of these scattered communities. The fishing and logging industries also became more up-to-date, losing their dependence on local support camps housing and providing for the workers.

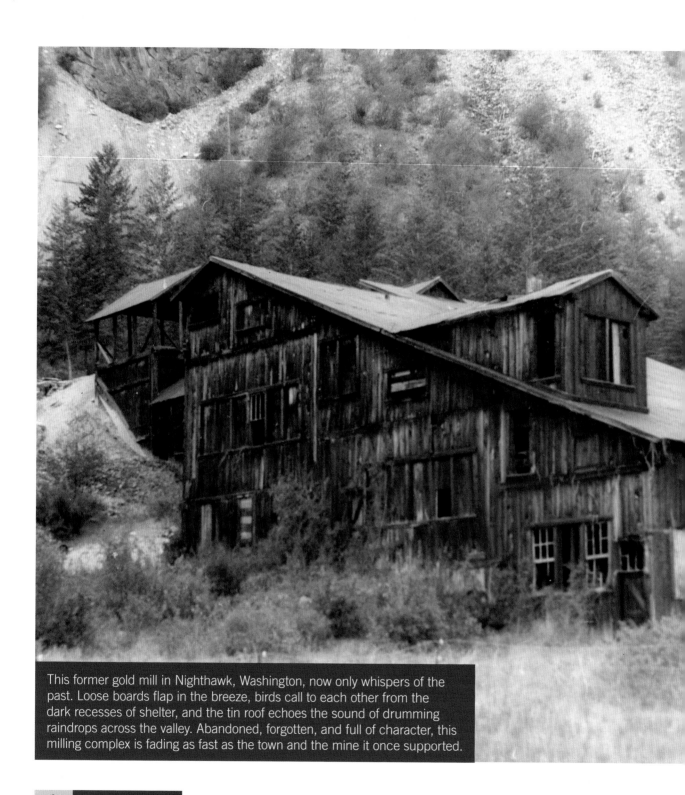

This former gold mill in Nighthawk, Washington, now only whispers of the past. Loose boards flap in the breeze, birds call to each other from the dark recesses of shelter, and the tin roof echoes the sound of drumming raindrops across the valley. Abandoned, forgotten, and full of character, this milling complex is fading as fast as the town and the mine it once supported.

**ABOVE** Inside one of the old stores in Hardman, Oregon, debris and rubble mark where customers once shopped for food, clothing, and other wants and needs.

**BELOW** Time has created personality in Elkhorn, Montana. The loss of shingles, windows, doors, and wooden siding boards allows rain and snow to enter; the lack of proper foundations, maintenance, and paint, as well as poor construction practices, cause buildings to deteriorate rapidly or tilt awkwardly one way or another.

# Bodie, Washington

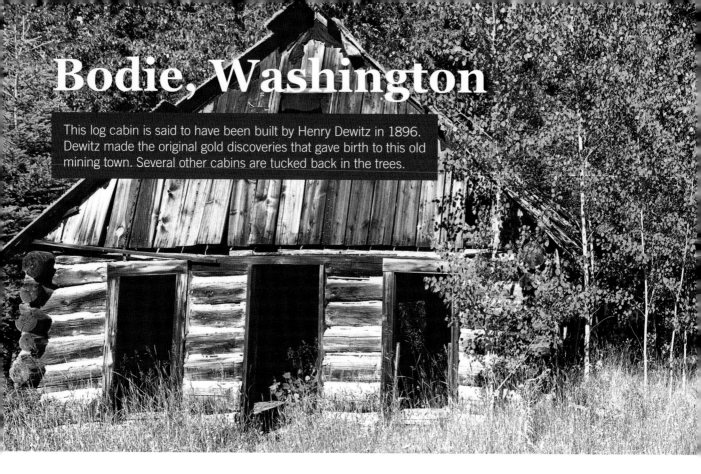

This log cabin is said to have been built by Henry Dewitz in 1896. Dewitz made the original gold discoveries that gave birth to this old mining town. Several other cabins are tucked back in the trees.

This classic old gold mining and milling town is located along Toroda Creek about 15 miles north-northeast of Wauconda. The original gold discoveries were made around 1888 a mile north of the confluence of Toroda and Bodie creeks by Henry Dewitz. His discovery caused a minor rush, and by 1890, a small mining camp had been established at the mouth of Bodie Creek. The name Bodie attached itself to the camp by 1896. In 1900, the camp relocated closer to the mine. A sawmill was also established at the mine site.

The town consisted of wood and log buildings holding businesses such as an assay office, a blacksmith, a bunkhouse, a cookhouse, a general store, a hotel, a livery, a restaurant, and a school. The latter is said to have also housed a saloon and an apartment after it was no longer used as an institution of learning. Dewitz and his brother sold their mine to the Wrigley brothers, who in 1902 built a large reduction mill at the mine site. That mill building was intentionally burned in 1962. Bodie itself continued to prosper until 1917, when the Bodie Mine closed. The town quickly followed suit. Then in the mid-1930s, prospectors came back, and Bodie operated until 1942, producing $1.25 million in gold. About half a dozen buildings still stand today at this road-accessible ghost town.

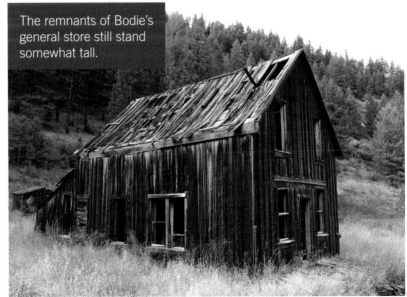

The remnants of Bodie's general store still stand somewhat tall.

# Molson, Washington

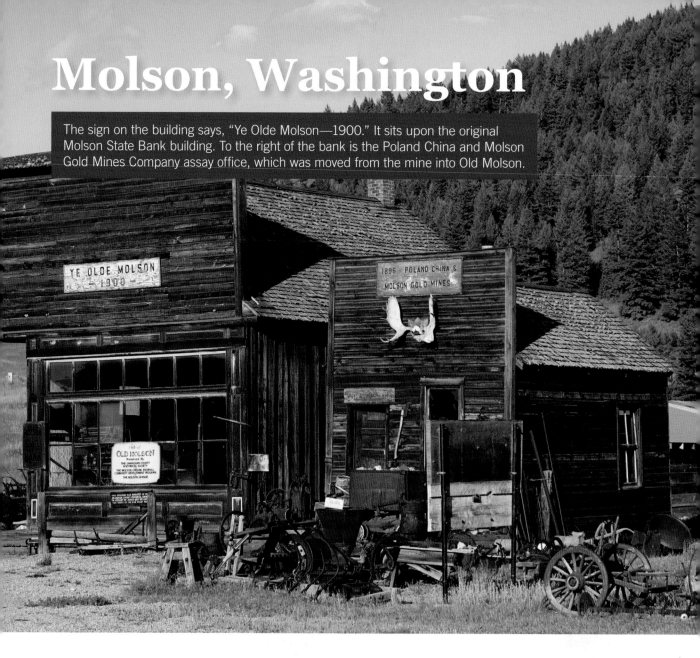

The sign on the building says, "Ye Olde Molson—1900." It sits upon the original Molson State Bank building. To the right of the bank is the Poland China and Molson Gold Mines Company assay office, which was moved from the mine into Old Molson.

**M**olson holds an interesting footnote among ghost towns: It was three overlapping town sites that were all occupied at the same time. Molson was established around 1900 about two miles south of the Canadian border, and northeast of Oroville. George Meacham and financier John Molson (of the Canadian brewing family) funded the

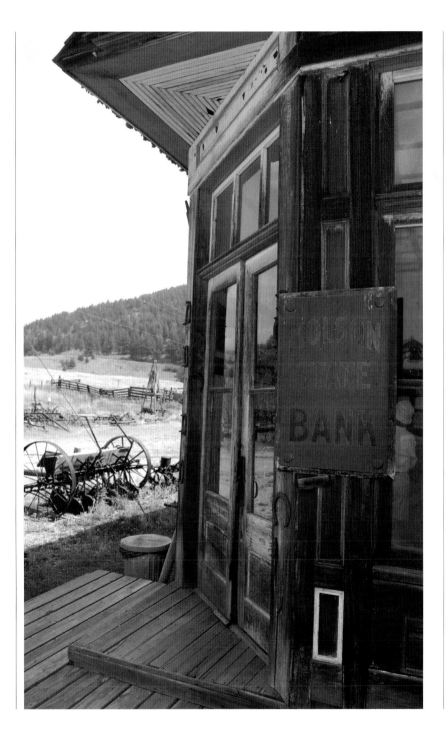

development as well as the Poland China Gold Mine, which was five miles east.

A town was platted, lots sold, and buildings built, including three general stores, three saloons, and the massive, wooden three-story Hotel Tonasket. In June 1901, however, Molson and Meacham pulled their money. Only 13 people remained where 300 had formerly lived.

But homesteaders soon arrived, and within a couple of years, stores reopened and some life returned. The Molson Townsite Company began redevelopment as rumors of a coming railroad gave the town the familiar feel of boom. But then J. H. McDonald filed for a homestead on land that included a portion of the developing Molson. On April 15, 1909, he posted a notice to vacate on that portion encroaching on his land. Litigation quickly followed.

The Molson storekeeper relocated to the railroad and was followed by the rest of the folks on McDonald's land. New Molson was born. For years, residents of Old and New bickered and fought. If a store would open at the site of one town, the other wanted one, too. Then in 1914, a school was built dead center between them. Center Molson was born.

It wasn't long after that, however, that the railroad was removed and all three parts of Molson folded. The last store closed in 1955. Numerous buildings, including museums, remain at all three sites.

**LEFT** Most of the buildings standing in Old Molson have been restored, relocated, or accurately rebuilt. The town's buildings and assorted other structures, along with all the gathered-up relics, make up an exciting open-air museum filled with the tangible history of this three-part town.

The faded sign at the top of this restored false front in Old Molson says, "Law and Order of the Highlands 1896–1972," while the lower sign reads, "Charles Dvorak Atty 1908–1910."

# Nighthawk, Washington

This old house is located at the Kaaba-Texas Mine, about a mile south of Nighthawk, along the west side of Allemandi Road and the Similkameen River.

Nighthawk was named after a bird common to the area. It wasn't a mining town per se, but a mining supply and transportation center that grew up around a ferry on the south side of the Similkameen River, 12 miles northwest of Oroville and five miles south of the Canadian border. The town got its start around 1900, and when the railroad reached it, it became a booming mining supply center.

In 1903, some of the local businesses included a brothel, a freighting company office, a general store, the two-story Nighthawk Hotel built by Ed McNull, a livery stable, a railroad depot, and several saloons. A small U.S. Customs Office

**ABOVE** The Nighthawk General Store also housed the post office and a Mobil gas station in 1969. By 2001, it had been converted into a private residence.

**LEFT** The Nighthawk Hotel was built in 1903 to serve those traveling to and from the mines in the area. It was much larger than most small towns with only 50 residents would require, yet it was well used.

may also have been present, although it is unclear whether this was at the town or if it was the same one that currently sits five miles to the north on the U.S./Canada border. The Nighthawk Mine perched on the side of a hill just south of town.

By the 1950s Nighthawk had faded, and the train was down to a couple of stops a week. The tracks were pulled out that same decade. By the 1970s, only the small general store remained in operation. Today Nighthawk is a photogenic collection of buildings, including the old two-story hotel, the schoolhouse, and cabins.

# Golden, Oregon

The Golden Mercantile also housed the town's post office. It was typical in smaller communities for the post office to operate from a corner of the general store or the lobby of a hotel rather than in its own standalone structure.

**G**olden, Oregon, is one of the earliest Western mining camps established as the California Gold Rush began. It was actually part of the mining boom that enveloped northwestern California and southwestern Oregon in 1850, the year the original placer gold deposits were discovered along Coyote Creek, about four miles east of today's Interstate 5 and just north of the Oregon/California state line.

The resources were quickly drained, and the boomers headed off to other, more promising locations along the Salmon River. Some 500 Chinese miners then moved onto the old placer workings and patiently panned and removed the remaining gold. When the Salmon River operations folded, however, many of

The Golden Mercantile store was built around 1896 by Schuyler Ruble. He sold to Columbus Bennett, who then sold to Harold McIntosh.

the previous miners came back. The Chinese then either sold their claims back to the original miners or, as some sources contend, were forced off their claims.

Around 1892 enough people were in the area to establish a small town. But by the 1920s, Golden began to limp, its energy gone and its economy in tatters. Today, the town is slowly being restored. Some of that restoration will include reconstruction of buildings no longer standing.

# Hardman, Oregon

This panoramic view of the once prosperous, bustling, agricultural town of Hardman dates to around 1905.

*Hardman, Or*

**T**his little agricultural ghost in north-central Oregon sits at the southern edge of the grasslands in southwestern Morrow County. It was the winner in a post office free-for-all scrap between a pair of "dogtowns." According to Lambert Florin in *Oregon Ghost Towns*, Raw Dog (which was originally called Dairyville) and Yellow Dog were rival stage stations a mile apart. In the 1870s, stages and various wagon trains would, depending on the driver's preferences, stop at either town. By the late 1870s, rumors of a coming post office caused the rivalry to increase. Since Raw Dog was a bit bigger, the dogfight ended when the post office landed there

**ABOVE** The splintering false front and decaying boardwalk at the old general store building lends a unique, desolate, modern-artish air to Hardman's remaining cluster of buildings.

**BELOW** Unhindered by endless, nearly treeless grain fields and dead houses with glassless window sockets, eastern Oregon's grassland prairie zephyrs zip through abandoned rooms of farm houses in Hardman.

in 1881. However, the postal authorities didn't like the name, so the post office was named after David Hardman, the landowner on whose farm the building was located.

Hardman grew, adding a hotel, an Independent Order of Odd Fellows (IOOF) Hall, a jail, a flour mill, a drugstore, a grocery store, churches, a school, and a community water pump, among other businesses. The town is said to have had 900 residents in the 1880s.

# Bonanza, Idaho

Aptly named, Bonanza is located along the Yankee Fork of the Salmon River, nine miles north of Sunbeam, and southwest of Challis. The original gold find here dates to as early as 1866, but despite flurries of discoveries, no boom occurred for a decade. In August 1876, three men found a rich, easy-to-work ledge. The General Custer Mine was staked, then after some brief litigation, the miners sold out for $286,000.

In 1876, Bonanza City began, and the following year it was platted, laid out, and had lots sold. Log buildings went up, two of the first being a store and a saloon, much to the delight of the local miners. A sawmill was built to supply cut lumber for construction.

By 1880, the population reached somewhere between 600 and 1,500, and the town had a café/dance hall, grocery stores, a hardware store, a hotel, a newspaper (*Yankee Fork Herald*), a post office, saloons, a school, and variety stores. At the General Custer Mine, a 30-stamp mill was completed in 1880, supported by a new town called Custer and its 300 people.

In 1889, a fire swept through Bonanza. Since Custer was growing and

thriving, many of the surviving businesses relocated there, and Custer soon counted about 600 residents. Another fire in 1897 sealed Bonanza's fate as a has-been. Custer now had the post office, the people, and the businesses—until 1910, that is, when the census found only 12 families to count.

Buildings remain at both Bonanza and Custer. The latter has a museum, and other buildings are being restored.

**ABOVE** Weathered fencing surrounds a grave in one of the two cemeteries that served both Bonanza and Custer.

**LEFT** Winter in Idaho's mountainous regions can be very cold, as demonstrated by the snow and icicles in this photo of an unidentified gentleman releasing water from behind a local log dam.

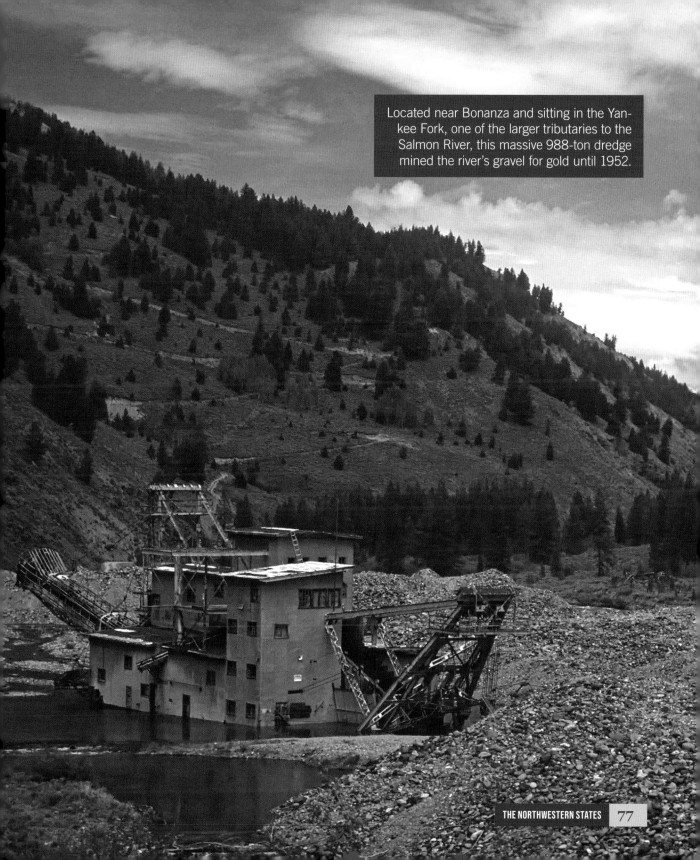

Located near Bonanza and sitting in the Yankee Fork, one of the larger tributaries to the Salmon River, this massive 988-ton dredge mined the river's gravel for gold until 1952.

# Chesterfield, Idaho

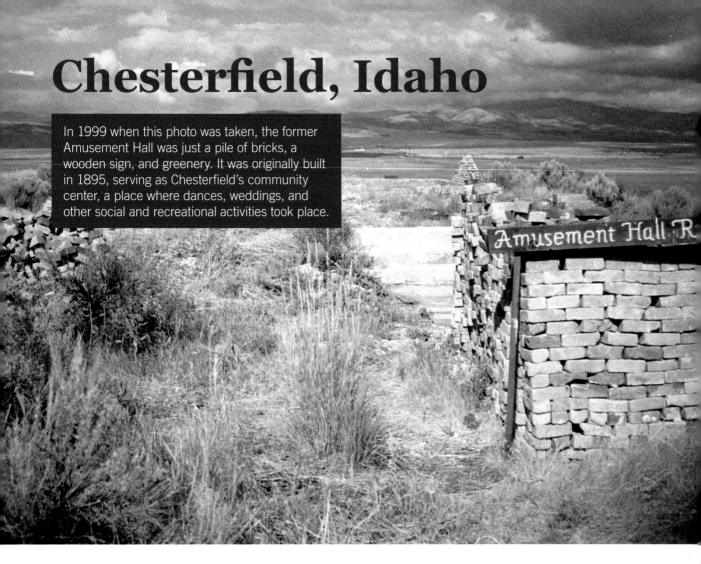

In 1999 when this photo was taken, the former Amusement Hall was just a pile of bricks, a wooden sign, and greenery. It was originally built in 1895, serving as Chesterfield's community center, a place where dances, weddings, and other social and recreational activities took place.

Amusement Hall R

C hesterfield's beginning comes with its namesake, a Mormon bishop named Chester Call, who visited the location in 1879. He and his nephew Christian Nelson felt this valley would make an excellent location for a town, so they spread the word, and a little town quickly developed. The two earliest structures here were a community meetinghouse and a nearby sawmill. Only four years later, Chesterfield had been surveyed, and lots had been sold.

**RIGHT** The Rugers arrived in Chesterfield around 1900, building their home by partially digging into the ground to save on construction costs. In 2009, reconstruction began, to be completed in summer 2010.

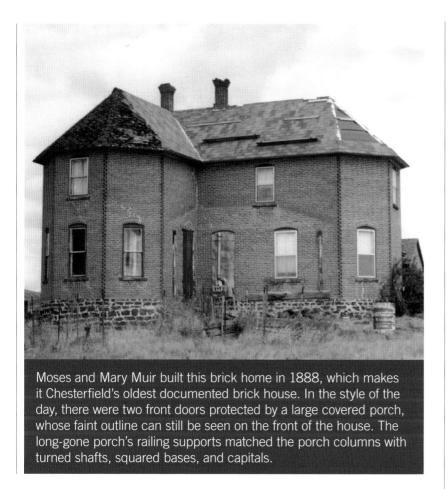

Moses and Mary Muir built this brick home in 1888, which makes it Chesterfield's oldest documented brick house. In the style of the day, there were two front doors protected by a large covered porch, whose faint outline can still be seen on the front of the house. The long-gone porch's railing supports matched the porch columns with turned shafts, squared bases, and capitals.

Construction began, with many of the buildings being built of brick.

In 1890, 339 people lived here. They were supported by a brick kiln, a church, a meetinghouse or community center, a school, a store, a tithing house, and other buildings.

The little community continued to grow, and by 1900, some 418 lived here. Times changed, however, and the town began to fade. Agriculture proved to be extremely tough in this isolated corner of Idaho, and even the self-reliant Mormons began to experience crop difficulties. Through the early 1900s, Chesterfield continued its slow decline.

# Silver City, Idaho

In 1863, the massive wooden Idaho Hotel was built in Ruby City, but in 1866 it was dismantled and moved to Silver City. The much-expanded hotel closed around 1942. An abandoned and derelict structure, it was purchased in 1972 by Edward Jagels, who spent the next 30 years restoring it.

The discovery of a placer deposit of an alloy of gold and silver along Jordan Creek on May 18, 1863, drew in prospectors. The Owyhee Placers, as they were known, were taken up quickly. A year later they were mostly exhausted.

On August 15, 1863, however, the Oro Fino quartz ledge was discovered, followed by the Morning Star, a silver ledge. Assays revealed high values. Word got out, and by the spring of 1864, Boonville, Ruby City, and Silver City had become booming mining camps.

The three towns grew quickly, and because Silver City had the best location, it grew the fastest. In 1867 Silver City was awarded the Owyhee County seat, which it held until 1935. This boom continued through the 1870s, and the streets were filled with hundreds of buildings all supporting the thousands of folks that called it home. Mining booms don't last forever, of course. By 1880 only 600 people remained, and Silver City continued to shrivel until 1942, when the mines closed down.

**LEFT** In this view of Silver City from the early 1900s, the dark cluster in the lower right-center is the Idaho Hotel. The school is the light-colored building peeking above the large white Masonic Hall in the center. On the knoll above and to the left of the school is the Catholic church.

**BELOW** In April 1959, the Owyhee Cattlemen's Association held their annual meeting at Silver City. The association has been active since 1878 and still represents more than 200 ranchers in the Owyhee County, Idaho, and the Malheur County, Oregon, areas.

# Elkhorn, Montana

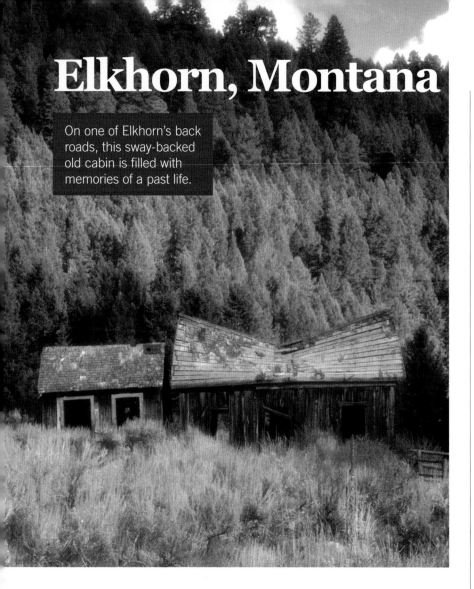

On one of Elkhorn's back roads, this sway-backed old cabin is filled with memories of a past life.

In 1870, silver was discovered nearby. Elkhorn grew slowly until the 1880s, when it boomed with churches, hotels, lodge halls, a post office (from 1884 to 1924), 14 saloons, stores, and 2,500 people. The mines faded, finally closing after producing some $14 million in gold and silver.

Most of the remaining 50 structures are privately owned, and a small handful of residents keep an eye on them. The two best buildings are the two-story lodge halls, which make up Elkhorn State Historic Park. Elkhorn sits at the end of a long dirt road in a forested bowl southeast of Helena. It boomed through the 1880s and 1890s and wasn't too badly affected by the silver panic of 1893.

By the turn of the 20th century, however, life slowed, the mines decreased production, and Elkhorn's boom followed the last outbound train. Because the town has never burned and has always had a few people, what remains makes this a real gem. The buildings are posted and well identified, so visitors can still enjoy them while remaining on the roads.

**RIGHT** During Elkhorn's boom years, hundreds of woodcutters lived at one end of town, their mules bringing in a constant supply of wood to be used as fuel to keep residents warm. Massive quantities of wood were also consumed by the silver mines and mills scattered around the hills above town.

Because of all the still-standing buildings, Elkhorn is one of the best ghost towns in Montana, let alone the country. All but two of the buildings in this state park, however, are privately owned and must be viewed from the street. The two state-owned buildings are open to visitors.

# Garnet, Montana

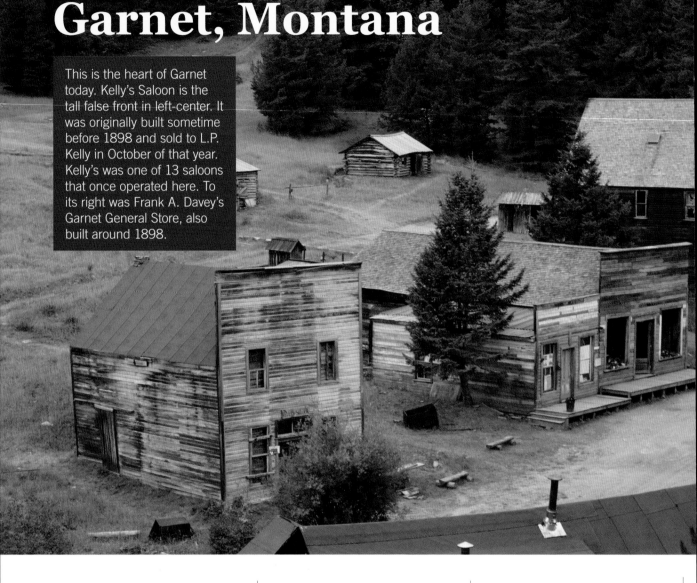

This is the heart of Garnet today. Kelly's Saloon is the tall false front in left-center. It was originally built sometime before 1898 and sold to L.P. Kelly in October of that year. Kelly's was one of 13 saloons that once operated here. To its right was Frank A. Davey's Garnet General Store, also built around 1898.

This old gold-mining town is located in the Garnet Mountains above Bearmouth, where the original placer gold discoveries were made in 1862 and were followed quickly by the discovery of lode mines. These mines pumped out more than $10 million in gold.

Garnet's structures of wood and logs were never built to last, most being plopped directly onto the ground without even the benefit of a foundation. And the

**ABOVE** Like Bodie, California, Garnet's elderly buildings are being stabilized and preserved as is, in a state of arrested decay.

**BELOW** The large building in the back right of the photo is the J. K. Wells Hotel, built in winter 1897. Behind the hotel and above the rear of the Davey Store is the blacksmith shop.

majority of them didn't last, either. Until they decayed away.

Garnet experienced two boom-bust cycles. The first was the decade from 1883 until 1893 when some 1,000 people lived in town and another 3,000 in the hills and valleys around it. The second boom occurred from 1898 through 1904, but by 1905, fewer than 200 people still called it home. A post office opened in 1896, before that second boom, and remained operational until 1928.

In 1912, the town suffered a disastrous fire. As it had already been in decline at that point, the community was never rebuilt, and the fire served as Garnet's funeral pyre. All that remains today are the BLM-restored structures that survived the conflagration.

# Granite, Montana

Though it looks like a wooden puzzle today, the once-busy Granite Mountain Mining Company mill processed ore from the Ruby Shaft, one of the richest mines in Granite.

**T**he chocolate-color, ragged wooden buildings that once housed saloons, general stores, hotels, and several thousand people in Granite mark yet another classic ghost town. The silver here was discovered on July 6, 1875, but there was no development of the mines until 1880.

Granite moved from the category of small mining camp to boomtown in November 1882 with a major silver discovery deep in the Granite Mine. That find precipitated a

**RIGHT** Only the side and rear walls remain of the Granite Miner's Union Hall. The building was erected in 1890 at a cost of $23,000 to be Granite's social center. It contained meeting rooms for lodges and the Miner's Union, union offices, and a library. Upstairs there was a large open room with a special dance floor for dances, operas, and theatrical productions.

building spree, when hotels, stores, and blocks of other buildings were added to the town's streetscape. In 1890, Granite had 1,310 people and had to institute water rationing. Two years later, the water problem was solved, and the population had increased to about 3,600. A bank, a brewery, a brothel, four churches, a two-story wooden hospital, various hotels, a three-story miner's union hall, a newspaper, a post office, and 18 saloons lined a long main street. Many of these buildings were open 24 hours a day.

The mine produced $30 million or more in silver, but then came 1893. The Silver Panic closed the mines, and Granite almost disappeared overnight as some 3,000 people headed west toward Philipsburg. At least that's the story. The reality, however, is that the crashing silver markets had already affected the mines, and they had begun slowing before the panic itself. An overnight exit of the town does make a good story, though, even if it's a stretch.

In 1898, a second burst of energy reopened some mines, and Granite enjoyed its second boom. When the mines closed again in 1901, however, Granite was relegated to the past.

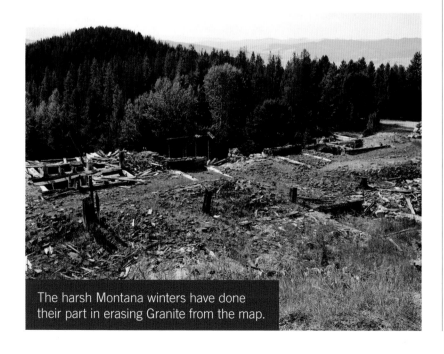

The harsh Montana winters have done their part in erasing Granite from the map.

In the late 1890s, the fading silver-mining town of Granite still sprawled across the hilly terrain above what is now Philipsburg. With some of the richest silver mines in Montana, Granite lived up to its nickname, "The Silver Queen."

GRANITE MT

# Bosler, Wyoming

Dead cars, dead buildings, dead grass, dead town: Welcome to Bosler, Wyoming. Abandoned in the early 1970s when the Lincoln Highway was supplanted by Interstate 80, Bosler's buildings languish on the frying-pan-flat Wyoming prairie.

The story of Bosler has its share of ups and downs. The town started life as a railroad shipping center and cattle town named after pioneer rancher Frank Bosler. In 1908 a big irrigation project was promised, and the post office, as well as a number of businesses, moved here.

When that project turned into vapor, however, the town faded out until the cross-country Lincoln Highway added Bosler to its collection of road towns in the 1920s.

During the 1930s Dust Bowl era, drought hurt the area, and Bosler dried up. But something brought a few people back, as the 1941 population was 264. Unfortunately, the 1941 Works Progress Administration guide doesn't say what may have brought that on, and none of the population figures since 1950 exceed 75 people.

Until Interstate 80 bypassed the town in 1972, Bosler

remained a thriving road town with a motel, a restaurant, a gas station, an automotive repair garage, a library, a school, a church, and other assorted businesses. After 1973, however, the Union Pacific closed its Bosler station and loading facility. And Bosler rolled up its sidewalks.

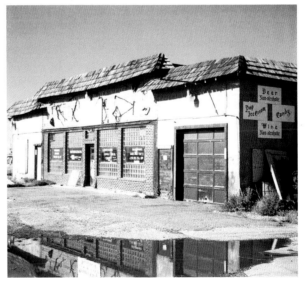

**ABOVE** The Bosler library was housed in this building. It probably closed along with the rest of the town in the early 1970s.

**LEFT** An old advertisement for Bosler's store appears on what may have been a storage building.

# Fort Laramie, Wyoming

These are the stabilized ruins of Fort Laramie's 12-bed hospital, which was built in 1873 and closed in 1890.

Located along the Oregon, California, Mormon, and Pony Express trails, Fort Laramie was strategically placed. It played an important role in the protection and supply of travelers along those roads as early as 1834 when it was a privately owned fur trading post called Fort William. In 1849 the U.S. government purchased the post and relocated and expanded it into a major military establishment to watch over the 50,000 people a year who used the Platte River trails.

Fort Laramie provided a welcoming travel respite from the rigors of the road, serving as a stagecoach and

**RIGHT** From 1834 to 1841, Fort William, also called Fort William-on-the-Laramie, was the only outpost of the U.S. military in this untamed region.

This is the restored lieutenant colonel's quarters, which was built in 1884. The lieutenant colonel was second in command at Fort Laramie, and his home was one of two nonduplex housing units on post—the commander's quarters was the other. Unlike the other buildings here, this structure was restored while a former resident, the son of the occupants who lived here in 1887 and 1888, was still alive.

Pony Express station. Major treaties with the Sioux were signed here, and for all the years the fort was a military outpost, it was never attacked—despite the fact that it had no protection beyond traditional fortress walls.

In 1890, the old post was decommissioned, and the land and all the structures were sold at auction to the public. In 1938 the federal government repurchased the property, and Fort Laramie National Monument saw daylight. Restoration began, and in 1960, this became Fort Laramie National Historic Site. It is located on the north side of the Laramie River, south of the North Platte River, and three miles southwest of the present town of Fort Laramie.

# Keeline/Jay Em, Wyoming

This photo of Keeline circa 1917 shows a much busier little town than visitors will find today. Some of the identifiable businesses include Bushnell's General Merchandise and Coal, Keeline Lumber Company yard, a hardware store, and the Fairview Hotel. Nowadays they are all gone.

Keeline started as a railroad shipping point for George A. Keeline's 4J Ranch. In 1910 Addison A. Spaugh platted and laid out the town of Keeline, honoring the pioneer rancher. Spaugh brought in a promoter and sold lots, and the town expanded. Some of the new businesses that came included a barbershop, a Chevrolet dealership, a hardware store, a lumberyard, and a restaurant. *The Keeline Record* newspaper was established in 1916 and published until 1923. The population may have reached 440, although evidence of that many people is hard to find in the scattered building shells and ruins that are now watched over by five people.

**RIGHT** One of the few remaining buildings at Keeline is the old school sitting on a low knoll. In 1940, there were still 101 residents, only a quarter of what there had been just 20–30 years before, but still almost 100 more than live there now. Today only the unused shells of the school, the post office, and several cabins and mobile homes remain.

The old Wolfe Garage on the left and gas station on the right are two of the identifiable buildings remaining in Jay Em. It operated as the Shoults Garage from 1928 to 1945 and was the Wolfe Garage from 1946 to 1960. Other remaining buildings include the lumber yard, the stone company, the general store, a hardware store, and a bank that operated from 1920 to 1945. On the second floor of these barn-shaped stores was a community hall.

The town of Jay Em was named after rancher James Moore's JM cattle brand. Moore was also once a Pony Express rider, and he settled in the area around 1869. The local post office and store were established in 1915 when they were moved from the ranch. In the 1930s, a gemstone cutting works was also present. This small ranching center is now a cluster of empty shells maintained and watched over by the 20 or so remaining townsfolk.

# THE MIDWESTERN STATES

**Other than small pockets such as the Black Hills, the tri-state corner southwest of Joplin, Missouri, and the iron and copper country around Lake Superior and Lake Michigan, this is a region richer in agricultural ghost towns than in mining ones. Look at any detailed map of these states: Thousands of tiny marker dots appear— especially in the eight less-urban states west of the Mississippi River. Most of these dots are dying farm towns.**

## The Big Question

If asked to name the cause of this demise, remaining residents of these sleepy, semi-ghost towns almost uniformly respond: "Big box retailer." Most mom-and-pop grocers, hardware stores, and other retail outlets can't obtain the same price breaks from wholesale suppliers, so their prices are generally higher. As a result, when Joe and Josephine Citizen drive the family jalopy to town to visit "Big Box" for cheaper goods, they will also take care of their banking, dining, and other shopping there. Mom-and-pop gas stations, restaurants, and small-town banks then lose that business, and as their clientele dries up, they eventually end up shutting down. And the cycle continues, customer by customer, store by store, year by year.

With the advent of huge corporate-owned megafarms, the numbers of smaller family farms decrease as people flee toward larger towns and cities. This exodus has resulted in a shrinking demand for schools, churches, and other social outlets in tiny farm towns. Cash-conscious government deems it more cost-effective to consolidate and close schools than to keep them open if they're only half filed. As more folks move away, schools close and church congregations shrink. Many churches find they can no longer support a full-time pastor, so circuit pastors become Sunday-only preachers without roots in the community. Multiple worship services shrink to one per week. Neighboring congregations share buildings and then start to disband, one by one. Abandoned schools and dead churches now share the landscape with block after block of Main Streets filled with empty brick storefronts. A dead town equals a newborn ghost town.

## The Shrinking Population

Another regionally common creator of ghost towns is

Built in 1914, the former home of the McGrew State Bank is on the west side of Main Street, across from The Pink Palace, in McGrew, Nebraska. In 1917, it was owned by Frank Jones, who also owned a cab service and the local Chevrolet dealership, but the bank failed in 1921. The building has been used for other purposes since.

relocation. When some towns were originally established, their placement may have been conveniently located for the local settlers. At a later date, however, when a railroad or highway was proposed for the area but—due to nearby rivers, steep grades, or even the refusal of landowners to sell, among other reasons—was built miles away, the town's location may have suddenly become less convenient. The new road or railroad might leave the town quite a distance off the now new-beaten path. Local merchants packed up and moved, rebuilding on or near the transportation corridor, leaving the original town site and most of its buildings to molder and decay.

River ports and railroad centers have been established and abandoned.

Copper-, coal-, and iron-mining areas boomed and waned. Logging, relocated county seats, and even utopian colonies grew and died. Each of these added their carcasses to the growing list of ghost towns.

The Heartland's declining rural communities make an interesting study. These scenarios are just a small part of the overall deterioration rural America has experienced since post–World War II prosperity created urban boomtowns and set off a mass migration to the cities. Some of the factors cited here may be more like nails sealing the coffin lid rather than the main event.

## Today's Reality

Yesterday's Heartland was in boom. Today's is not. Traveling back roads and scenic byways affords

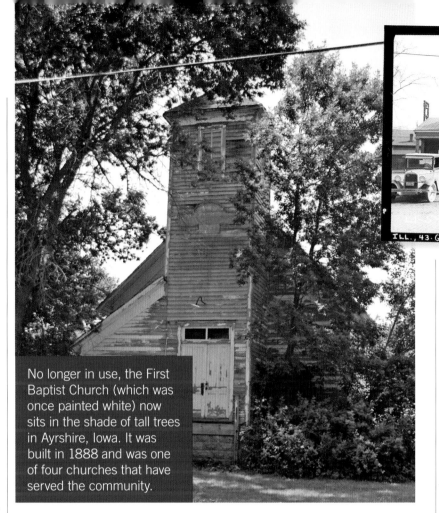

ILL., 43·GALA, 10-1          HABS

**ABOVE** The first floor of this old market building in Galena, Illinois, once bustled with the sounds of commerce, the sweet smell of baked goods, and colorful items arrayed by various vendors to provide the town's residents a one-stop shopping experience.

No longer in use, the First Baptist Church (which was once painted white) now sits in the shade of tall trees in Ayrshire, Iowa. It was built in 1888 and was one of four churches that have served the community.

casual travelers plenty of opportunity to experience the real soul of America's Heartland ghosts. Explore towns whose two or three blocks of Main Street are filled with unoccupied buildings. Listen to the ghosts of the past as they whisper stories of hardy pioneers. Smell the clean scent of agriculture wafting on the breeze. Allow the gaze to linger on the weathered bricks of Sacred Heart School. Trace the fading, gilt letters spelling out Dry Goods & Notions on the dirty storefront windows of the abandoned Deer Creek Mercantile Company general store.

Loll in the shade cast by the sagging wooden canopy, and watch the mama spider weaving her web between the support posts. Focus on the past. Hear the *kaching* of the massive brass cash register. Revel in the cheerful shouts and cries of children playing on the now rusty slides and swings at the overgrown park across the street. Listen to farmers talking shop while unloading freshly picked produce at the local market.

Slammed by the Great Depression and devastated by the Dust Bowl of the 1930s, many tiny towns in the central states, such as Frontenac, Minnesota, lost their battle to live as citizens escaped to the cities, leaving behind desiccated hopes and dried-up dreams.

**ABOVE** The 1880s through the 1920s were a period of optimistic growth throughout the region. Family farms and supporting towns grew faster in places such as Foss, Oklahoma, than did wheat during a warm spring. Substantial buildings were built, many of which remain as monuments to these hopes.

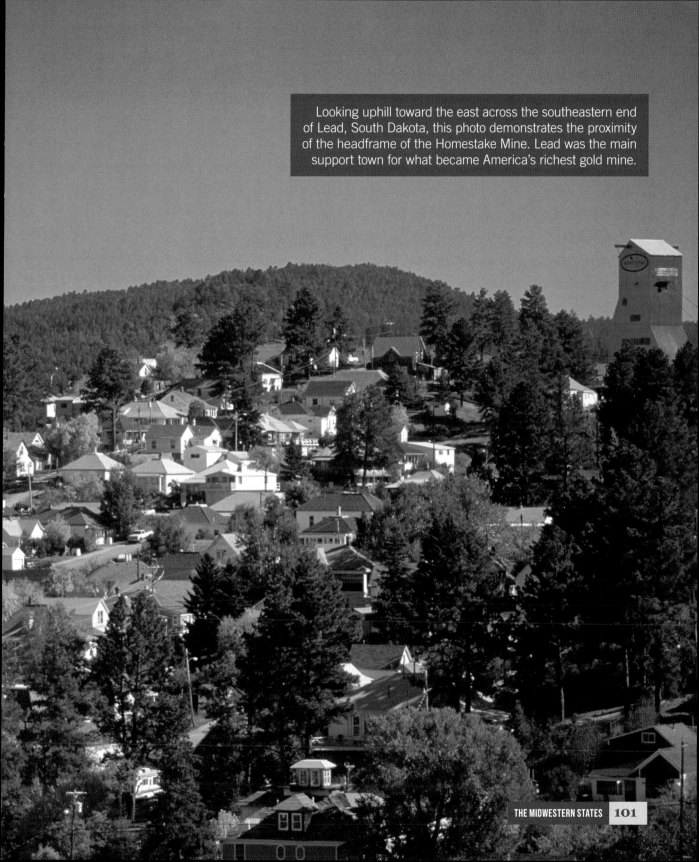

Looking uphill toward the east across the southeastern end of Lead, South Dakota, this photo demonstrates the proximity of the headframe of the Homestake Mine. Lead was the main support town for what became America's richest gold mine.

# Farmtowns of North Dakota

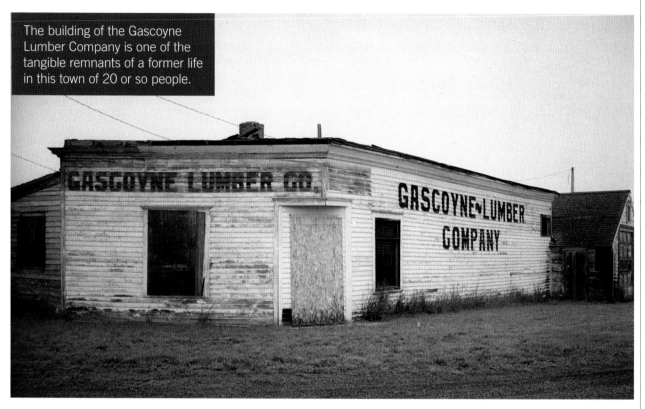

The building of the Gascoyne Lumber Company is one of the tangible remnants of a former life in this town of 20 or so people.

Scattered across the top of the semi-arid High Plains are hundreds, if not thousands, of dead and dying farm towns barely clinging to life. Decades ago, promises brought people. But the weather and the crashing economy of the 1930s drove them out.

Amidon, Bucyrus, and Gascoyne are just a few of the places now communing with ghosts. Studentless schools, spectral churches, vacant stores, and moneyless shells of banks mark death and abandonment on the wind-blown prairie.

In the early 1900s, railroads and homesteaders created a booming economy with towns popping up all over

**ABOVE** This postcard of Gascoyne was mailed from the town in April 1911. The settlement was originally established along the railroad in 1907 as Fischbein, but the name was changed to Gascoyne in 1908. As growth and prosperity occurred, large homes and a main street lined with businesses quickly gave an air of permanence. The mid-1930s ushered in decline, a state of affairs that has continued to this day. The post office closed in 1982, leaving Gascoyne a hollow shell of what it once had been.

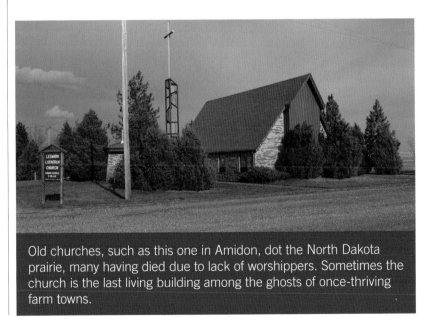

Old churches, such as this one in Amidon, dot the North Dakota prairie, many having died due to lack of worshippers. Sometimes the church is the last living building among the ghosts of once-thriving farm towns.

the prairie. Amidon arrived in 1910, grabbed the county seat of brand-new Slope County in 1915, and quickly boasted a school, banks, churches, a hotel, a restaurant, a movie theater, newspapers, a bowling alley and pool hall, a gas station, an automobile dealership, an undertaker, a barber, a lumberyard, stores of all kinds, and 162 residents in 1930.

Bucyrus began in 1908. Early businesses included a hotel, a restaurant, a Lutheran church, a post office, a bank, a railroad depot, a newspaper, a barber, a drugstore and doctor office, a school, lumberyards, a feed store, various other stores, blacksmiths, and a 1930 population of 124.

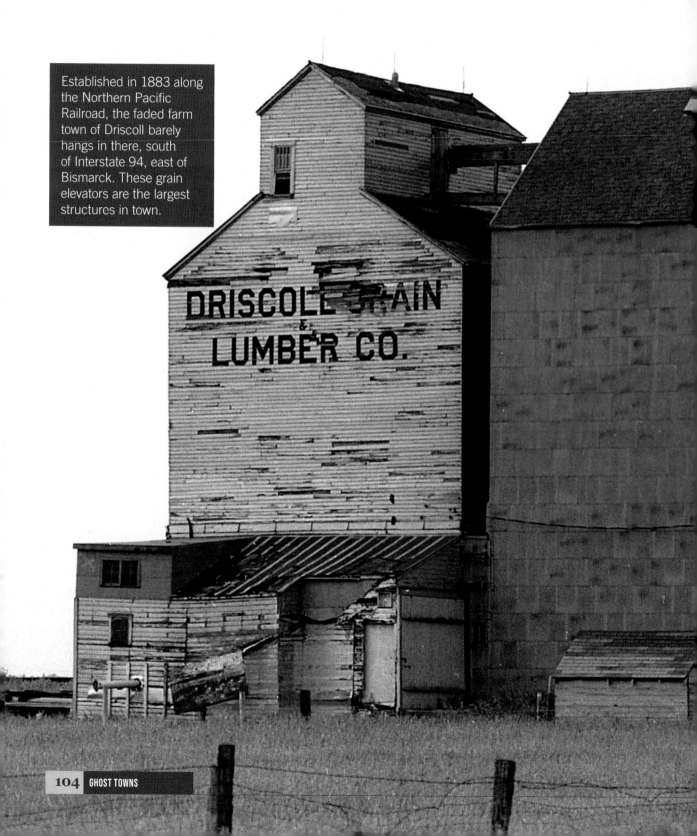

Established in 1883 along the Northern Pacific Railroad, the faded farm town of Driscoll barely hangs in there, south of Interstate 94, east of Bismarck. These grain elevators are the largest structures in town.

**ABOVE** Cleveland was founded in June 1882, also along the Northern Pacific Railroad, about 25 miles west of Jamestown. The town grew quickly, adding a post office and other businesses. The ruffle of excitement soon faded, however, and by 1884, Cleveland was a has-been. But in 1900 it was rediscovered: The post office reopened, and the sound of hammers once again echoed across the town. The 1920 census counted 341 residents. Unfortunately, a slow decline began, and by 1930, the population had sagged to 273. In 2020, the Census Bureau estimated only 57 people remaining. Along the west side of Euclid Avenue (Cleveland's main street) is a vacant bank, a grocery store, and the two-story town hall that housed offices upstairs and a dance hall/community center downstairs.

Gascoyne was the last of the three, incorporating in 1911. It had grain elevators, a general store, a post office, a school, a lumberyard, a bowling alley, and 97 people in 1930.

Drought, the Dust Bowl, and World War II sucked away employable people. These once-bustling little towns filled with promise are now filled with dead buildings and lost memories in a land that seems to eat its people, eat its buildings, and eat its towns.

# The Black Hills of South Dakota

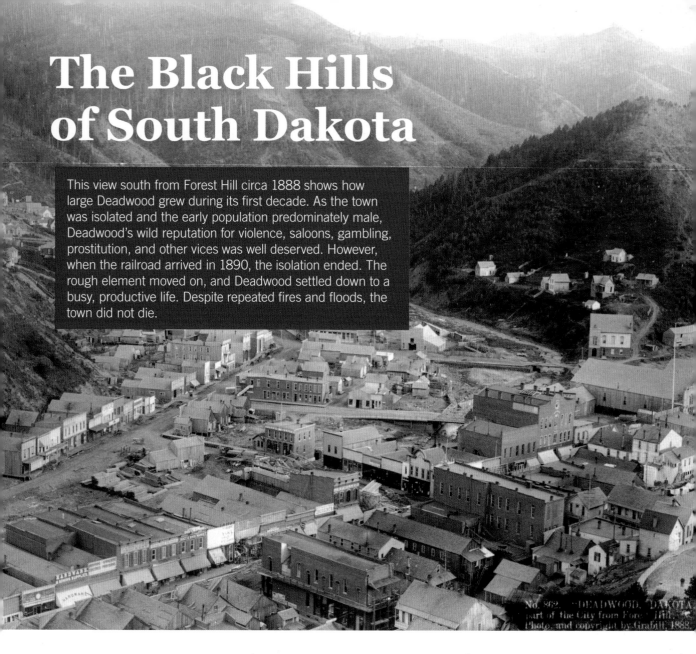

This view south from Forest Hill circa 1888 shows how large Deadwood grew during its first decade. As the town was isolated and the early population predominately male, Deadwood's wild reputation for violence, saloons, gambling, prostitution, and other vices was well deserved. However, when the railroad arrived in 1890, the isolation ended. The rough element moved on, and Deadwood settled down to a busy, productive life. Despite repeated fires and floods, the town did not die.

No. 862. "DEADWOOD, DAKOTA." part of the City from Forest Hill. Photo. and copyright by Grabill, 1888.

**G**old, gunfighters, and blood! Lakota Sioux, George Armstrong Custer, Calamity Jane, and Wild Bill Hickock!

A vivid history filled with colorful personalities enhances the mystique of South Dakota's Black Hills. Substantially more than

1,000 ghost towns have made their appearance in these hills called Paha Sapa by the Lakota Sioux. In the summer of 1874, while searching for a location to plant a military post, a party led by Lieutenant Colonel George Armstrong Custer discovered gold. This find created a massive gold rush and conflict with the Native American inhabitants. It ultimately resulted in Custer and his entire regiment's demise on June 17, 1876, in southeastern Montana, just to the west of the Black Hills.

Once the bottle was uncorked, however, miners swept in, much to the chagrin of the Lakota. In 1875 some 800 white miners were concentrated in three major towns—Custer, Deadwood, and Hill City. A year later, that population had exploded to more than 10,000, for four years of frenzy. Gold was yanked from the ground. Towns popped up

Lying in the heart of the Black Hills, Mystic is one of several great little ghosts that still have standing buildings. It also has a few ruins, foundations, and historic structures such as this old church building.

everywhere, disappearing again as the restless miners moved on.

Left today are hundreds of ghost towns with tangible remains. Deadwood was saved from ghostdom by tourists and gambling.

Lead (pronounced *leed*) had the magnificent Homestake Mine. Custer and Hill City had location. Other towns, such as Mystic, Rochford, and Central City, are not totally abandoned and offer mini-populations and mini-clusters of colorful buildings.

**ABOVE** When gambling was approved (again) in 1989, scores of casinos moved into empty buildings and quickly supplanted mining from the task of bringing in the gold. Revenue obtained from gambling is used by the city to continue its preservation efforts.

**LEFT** Filled with excellent examples of well-tended, late 19th-century architecture, today's Deadwood relishes its historic past. In fact, in 1964, the entire city was declared a National Historic Landmark.

# McGrew, Nebraska

Ora Adcock built the McGrew Mercantile Company stores, which today anchor the west side of Main Street, in 1912. The bank building is just out of the frame to the right of the brick store. Adcock opened for business as a general store, expanding and adding new buildings as business increased.

I n the late morning, birds chirp in trees, vainly trying to cast feeble shade over vacant buildings in the dry husk of what once passed for downtown. The gap-toothed row of empty buildings on Main Street recalls the teens and '20s, an era when McGrew prospered with an automobile dealership and repair garage, a bank, a barbershop, a blacksmith, a butcher, a café, a church, a creamery, several general stores, a grain elevator, a hardware store, a hotel, a lumber and coal yard, a newspaper (called *The Wasp*), a post office, a railroad depot, a saloon, a

**RIGHT** In April 1912, a Presbyterian church was established in McGrew. A building was erected, and services were held until early 1971. The building didn't sit vacant long after that, however, as in May of that year, Platte Valley Bible College lent a hand, and the McGrew Community Church opened its doors. In 1986, it was renamed the Oregon Trail Chapel.

Within the first decade after being established in 1911, McGrew experienced rapid growth, quickly becoming home to between 400 and 500 people. In that same decade, a large two-story masonry hotel was added to the expanding collection of businesses. Today the hotel no longer operates, but the building has become a popular tavern called the McGrew Lounge, or better known as the Pink Palace.

school, a stockyard, a sugar beet dump, and between 400 and 500 people.

Built in 1920, the magnificent brick school building that once echoed with the excited shouts of children heading out for recess now just amplifies the quiet. The only other buildings in use are the church (built in 1912) and the squat, red-trim, double-door fire station. Everything else, including the 1914 McGrew State Bank, the automotive repair garage, the 1912 McGrew Mercantile Company's General Merchandise block, and the post office (discontinued in 1986) dozes in the warm Nebraska sunshine. Memories hang thick in the air here: memories of when McGrew was a prosperous agricultural community sitting between the railroad and the North Platte River.

# Englewood, Kansas

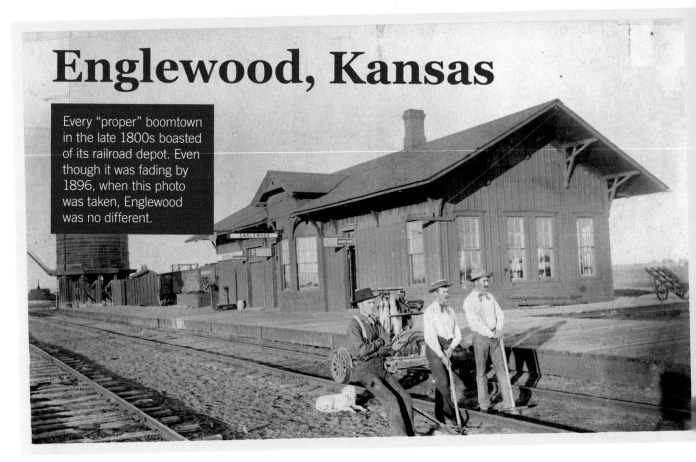

Every "proper" boomtown in the late 1800s boasted of its railroad depot. Even though it was fading by 1896, when this photo was taken, Englewood was no different.

Sitting athwart the cattle trail between Texas and Dodge City, Englewood became a must stop for cattle drovers trailing north toward Dodge. Atypical of most cattle towns, the hardest drink legally obtainable was cider, but that didn't seem to dampen anyone's spirits. Collapse walked hand-in-hand with drought and the economic depression of 1893, however. Farmers lost their land. The foreclosing banks failed. Land titles went into disarray. Englewood foundered, and dreams of eclipsing Dodge City disappeared.

In 1906, Colonel Clarence D. Perry offered a portion of his Claremont Ranch to give Englewood a chance at clear-titled rebirth. That offer was accepted by the townsfolk, and a new plat was filed.

Two years later, however, while "New Town" was in the midst of another boom, fire ripped through the entire western half of the business district. Englewood's spirit died with the ashes, its drive destroyed. By 2020, only 58 people remained in New Town. Nearby "Old Town" became a forgotten relic. Englewood's business district has since imploded. The former downtown core straddling a 100-foot-wide dirt main street is in shambles.

**ABOVE**
No longer pumping gas, this 1960s-era gas station sits right on the corner of U.S. 283 and Claremont Street, the main street of "New Town." By 2007, the gas pumps shown here had been removed.

In this photograph from the early 1900s, Samuel G. Hink stands in front of his single-story Claremont Street shoe repair business. Next door, the center two-story structure houses "Peter Schuttler Wagons." And next door to the left is another two-story building housing an interesting combination of businesses: "H. C. Power & Co., Hardware, Furniture, Undertaking." Today, these early-1900s buildings along the main street of "New Town" are long gone.

# Picher, Oklahoma

**L**ead-zinc mines were discovered here in 1914. Almost overnight, Picher and Ottawa County became boomtown central. From World War I through the 1920s, when Picher's mines peaked, 50 percent of the world's zinc came from here. The city was interspersed with massive underground mines, mills, and mushrooming piles of mining debris called chat. Little attention was given to future environmental concerns.

With World War II and its massive appetite for lead and zinc, Picher's population exploded, possibly reaching 16,000 or even 20,000. After the war, however, mining tanked, and Picher's days seemed to be numbered. The largest mines closed by 1957, and the last little one shut down in 1970.

During the 1990s, elevated lead content was found in the children of Picher. Tar Creek was heavily polluted. Winds stirred up toxic dust clouds from the chat piles, and cave-ins threatened buildings. Weeds, shrubs, and broken windows created an ominous air. The federal government stepped in, classifying the Picher-Cardin area as a Superfund site. In 2007, the *Washington Post* provided Picher's future epitaph with this headline: "A Tainted Mining Town Dies as Residents Are Paid to Leave."

The 1,640 "lead heads" and "chat rats" counted in 2000 have been evicted, and on June 30, 2009, Picher was officially abandoned. The post office closed in July, and the city was disincorporated on September 1, 2009.

In addition to a tornado, environmental disaster, and abandonment, Picher also suffers from what might be called "dropsy." Massive sinkholes caused by mine subsidence have opened up, creating serious safety hazards. Get an idea of the size of this hole by comparing it to the person standing on its lip for perspective.

**LEFT**
In the late afternoon of May 10, 2008, a tornado with winds estimated in the range of 170 miles per hour ripped through Picher, flattening or extensively damaging some 20 blocks of town, killing six people including a baby, and injuring another 150. A disaster declaration was made, but because of the federal buyouts in progress, no funds were released for repair or rebuilding. Victims of property loss or damage could only use the money for help in relocating.

# Frontenac, Minnesota

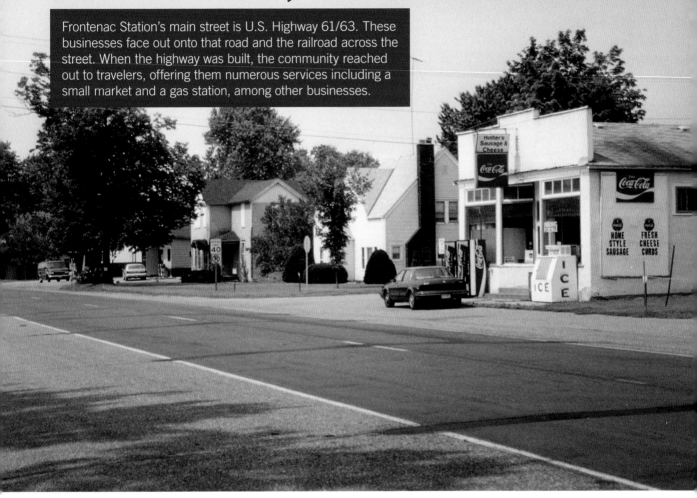

Frontenac Station's main street is U.S. Highway 61/63. These businesses face out onto that road and the railroad across the street. When the highway was built, the community reached out to travelers, offering them numerous services including a small market and a gas station, among other businesses.

Sixty miles southeast of St. Paul, along the west side of Lake Pepin and on the Mississippi River, James "Bully" Wells established an American Indian trading post in 1839. In the 1850s, he sold most of his land to Evert Westervelt. While out hunting, Israel and Lewis Garrard of Cincinnati, Ohio, fell in love with the beauty of this area, and they joined forces with Westervelt in 1857. Together, the three platted and laid out a small town called Westervelt. Two years later, the two Garrards, along with their brothers Kenner

**ABOVE** Built in 1867, the majestic Lakeside Hotel was the first of several large hotels built to serve visitors to Frontenac. Originally a two-story warehouse, once the building was remodeled, it became the first resort hotel in that part of the country. Because of the Lakeside Hotel, Frontenac became a magnet for vacationers in the middle-to-late 1800s.

**BELOW** A modern outdoor motorized sports equipment dealership resides in this fancy-fronted antique building that may have had a previous life as an old bank.

and Jeptha, bought out Westervelt and changed the name of their town to Frontenac.

The railroad was due to come through in the 1870s, but the Garrards refused to sell any land, so Frontenac was bypassed. A station was built a couple of miles away, and the small community that developed around it was christened Frontenac Station. But with the railroad came a decrease in use of steamships, which resulted in diminished river traffic.

In 1901, Israel Garrard passed away, but his legacy continues in the ethereal quiet and beauty of this place. Parts of Frontenac have been designated the only "Historic District" in the state, and much of this area has become Frontenac State Park.

# Grasston Area, Minnesota

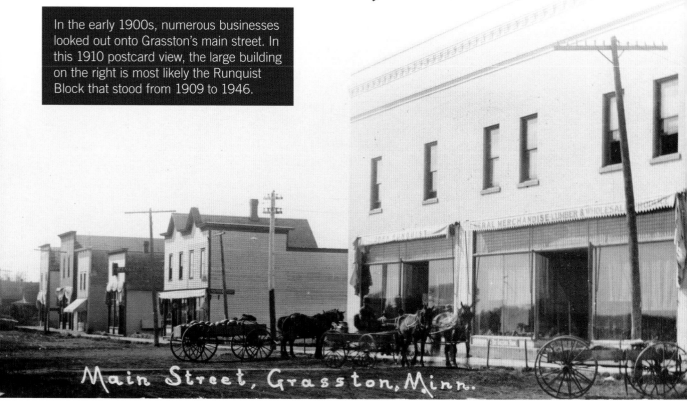

In the early 1900s, numerous businesses looked out onto Grasston's main street. In this 1910 postcard view, the large building on the right is most likely the Runquist Block that stood from 1909 to 1946.

Main Street, Grasston, Minn.

Grasston's population has dropped from 229 in 1930 to 158 in 2010, while the commercial district now has more sidewalk and foundations poking out of grassy, vacant lots than it has standing buildings. Grasston was laid out on June 6, 1899, when the railroad came through and built a station. Some of the other businesses in town included a couple of churches, the large 1901 Swan Hotel, a livery stable, a lumberyard, a post office, a school, and other typical small-town businesses. Grasston was also home to a 14-piece band and a men's chorus. The town was incorporated on October 21, 1907.

Today's Grasston contains an empty false front, the post office, the Grasston City Hall, an old gas station that in the late 1990s was converted to a café, a couple of churches, a fire station, an auto repair garage, a feed

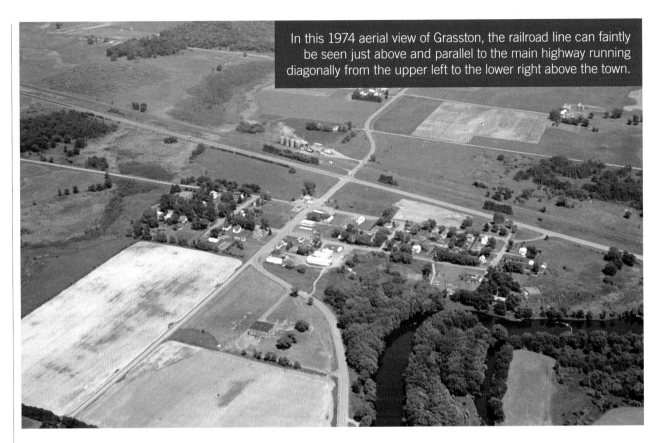

In this 1974 aerial view of Grasston, the railroad line can faintly be seen just above and parallel to the main highway running diagonally from the upper left to the lower right above the town.

mill, a grain elevator, and a handful of homes.

Just a few miles to the north is another dying little 100-person farm town named Henriette. It hails from the same era and has a similar number of colorful old buildings remaining from the boom days.

The present-day fire hall in Grasston replaced an older, white false-front building that still stands but is not being used.

# Farmtowns in Southwest Iowa

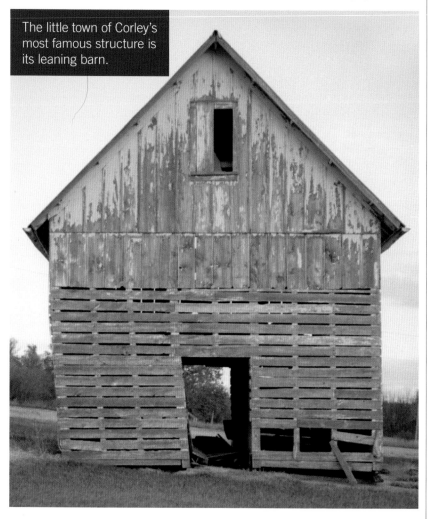

The little town of Corley's most famous structure is its leaning barn.

**L**ying east of the Missouri River, north of the Missouri state line, and south of Interstate 80 is a lost world. Here in southwestern Iowa, scores of dead and dying farm towns are a microcosm of what's happening throughout America's Heartland.

Each of these towns has its own personality and its own few remaining citizens clinging to hope that the town will somehow come back, reversing a more than 60-year decline. These towns have schools that have been transformed into homes and apartments, stores converted to storage buildings or left empty, and fading advertisements painted on brick walls of long-forgotten stores, hawking forgotten goods and services. Grain silos stand sentinel over decaying main streets where the only active businesses are often the ubiquitous taverns. Rusted-out pickups rattle up and down potholed main streets while bicycles

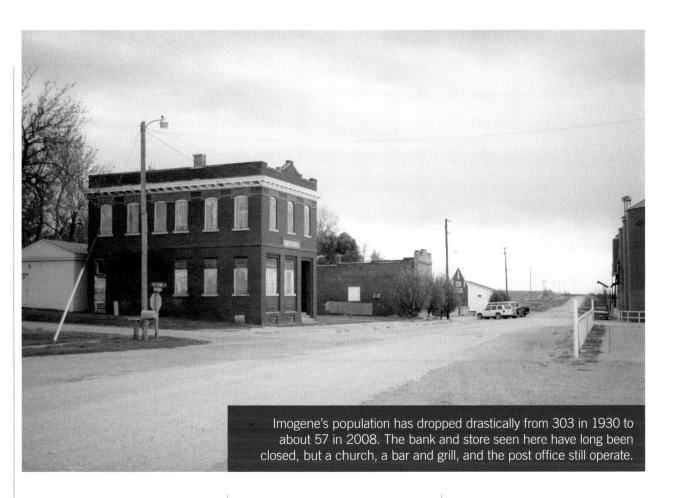

Imogene's population has dropped drastically from 303 in 1930 to about 57 in 2008. The bank and store seen here have long been closed, but a church, a bar and grill, and the post office still operate.

toting kids zip through the dust. Other children play cowboy in weedy, overgrown parks. Ancient, vacant, tree-covered homes sit next door to well-maintained Victorians.

Stretching beyond the ragged edges of dispirited communities, undulating fields of corn march up and down the rolling countryside. Cornfields periodically yield to open space, allowing another tiny town to wallow in its former glory and deepening memories. Two-lane country roads once bringing life-giving commerce flow past faded signs welcoming nonexistent travelers to dead motels, closed stores, and busted banks. Other dead towns sit alongside railroad tracks, no longer even warranting a flag stop for highballing trains. Hope still flickers, and memories flow as thick as Iowa's August air.

**ABOVE** This tiny false front, labeled "Hotel," marks Mineola, a little agricultural town whose population hasn't varied much since 1900. Its antique Main Street is lined with whitewashed buildings, some housing active businesses, some turning their empty storefronts out for all to see.

**RIGHT** The Mills County German Bank was established in 1903 to serve the predominantly German population of Mineola and Mills County.

C. F. ROENFELD, President          CHAS. F. NIPP, Cashier

## Mills County German Bank

MINEOLA,     -     -     IOWA

We solicit your business and offer you such facilities as are usually extended by an obliging and carefully managed bank.   -   -   -

——DIRECTORS——
Mrs. Henry Nipp,  H. F. Kruse,  C. F. Roenfeld,  L. M. Lord,  C. F. Nipp

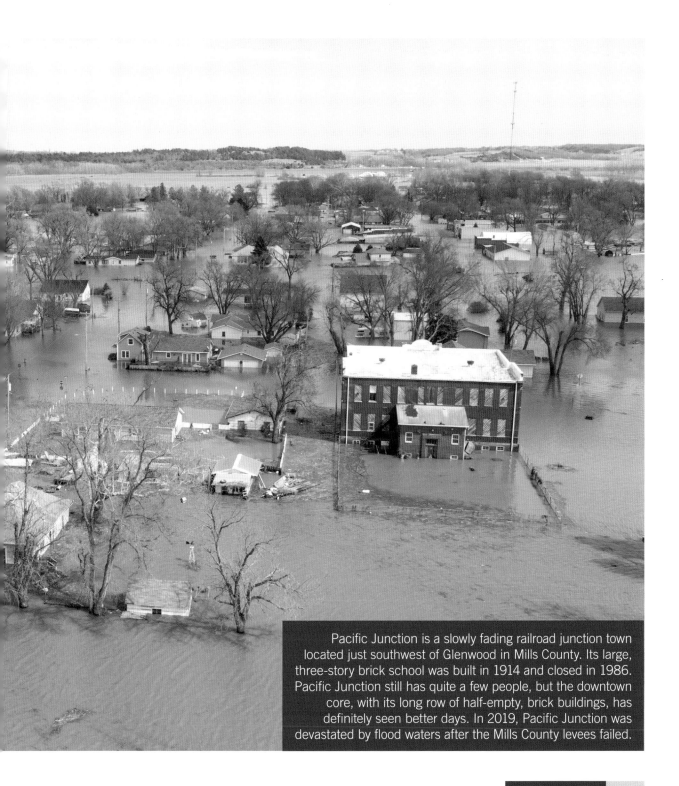

Pacific Junction is a slowly fading railroad junction town located just southwest of Glenwood in Mills County. Its large, three-story brick school was built in 1914 and closed in 1986. Pacific Junction still has quite a few people, but the downtown core, with its long row of half-empty, brick buildings, has definitely seen better days. In 2019, Pacific Junction was devastated by flood waters after the Mills County levees failed.

# Ayrshire, Iowa

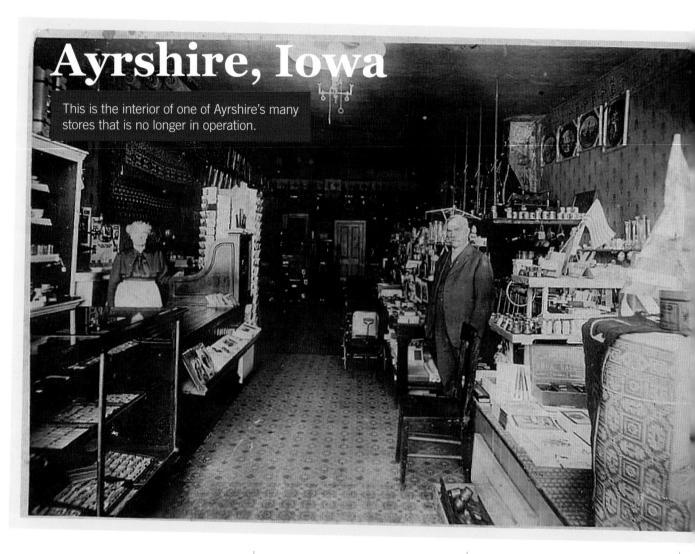

This is the interior of one of Ayrshire's many stores that is no longer in operation.

The Chicago-Northwestern Railroad breathed life into Ayrshire when it pushed through in 1882. Within two years, 35 people lived here, but that changed quickly, as settlement of Ayrshire ramped up. The population reached 343 in 1930, but it has dropped steadily since, down to an estimated 133 in 2020.

During the 1930s, businesses included at least four churches (Baptist, Catholic, Lutheran, and Methodist-Episcopal), a Catholic school and a public school, two automobile garages, a billiard/beer hall, a blacksmith, a coal and lumber business, a confectioner, a creamery, a drugstore, a farm implements purveyor, several gasoline filling stations, two general stores, a furniture store, a grain elevator, grocery stores, a hardware store, a harness shop, a hotel and restaurant, a meat market, a weekly newspaper, a post office, a railroad depot, a standalone restaurant, a telephone exchange, and a baseball team.

**RIGHT**
Construction of the Sacred Heart Catholic School began in 1920 but wasn't completed until the summer of 1924. The last class was held in 1968.

Today, only a handful of businesses remain, interspersed with vacant buildings such as the American Legion Hall, a bank, a bar, three of the churches, city hall, the grain elevator, a hair salon, the post office, the telephone company office, and the Silver Lake Township Hall. The public high school built in 1920 closed in the mid-1980s.

Downtown Ayrshire is home to this brick building that serves two purposes: housing the Ayrshire Office of Laurens State Bank on the left and the post office—in front of the car on the side street—to the right. The bank branch opened in 1931 and ultimately relocated here, leaving an empty shell elsewhere in town. The post office has been in operation since around 1884.

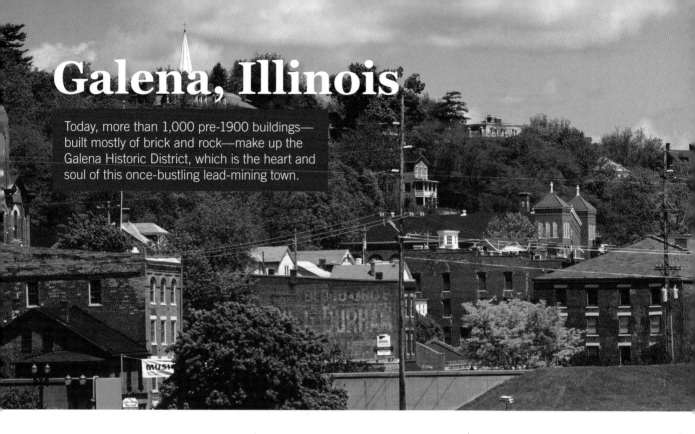

# Galena, Illinois

Today, more than 1,000 pre-1900 buildings—built mostly of brick and rock—make up the Galena Historic District, which is the heart and soul of this once-bustling lead-mining town.

G alena is a unique, active, historic community fully capitalizing on its historic past. Prior to the Civil War, it was in the heart of America's main lead-mining region. The first lead was shipped from the area's mines in 1816, and a decade later Galena was established. In just one year, 1854, Galena's mines shipped 54 million pounds of lead, more than 80 percent of the country's total!

That same year, however, fire decimated the city. Rebuilding was quick, but a second conflagration in

**BELOW** The panorama of Galena in 1915 displays a vibrant town that has held on to its heritage.

**BELOW** In 1859 city clerk Alexander J. Jackson began construction of the home below. In 1865 he sold it to a group of prominent Republican residents who presented it to hometown hero General Ulysses S. Grant, thanking him for his role in winning the Civil War. Before the war, Grant and his family lived in Galena, and he worked in his father's store. Grant and his family lived in this home until 1868, when he was elected president.

1856 resulted in the city council passing an ordinance requiring all new buildings to be constructed of brick or stone. As the Civil War wound up, Galena's economy unwound, quickly losing its number-one ranking in the lead-mining industry, in transportation, and in regional marketing. From there, the town rapidly faded through the 1860s.

For the next 100 years, Galena hung in there— barely. Then came the 1960s and early 1970s: City refugees flocked here, liked what they saw, and stayed. Today, Galena's historic district is rated the best example of Victorian architecture in the Heartland, with the historic downtown business district having 85 percent of its buildings listed on the National Register of Historic Places. Not a bad legacy!

# Old Shawneetown, Illinois

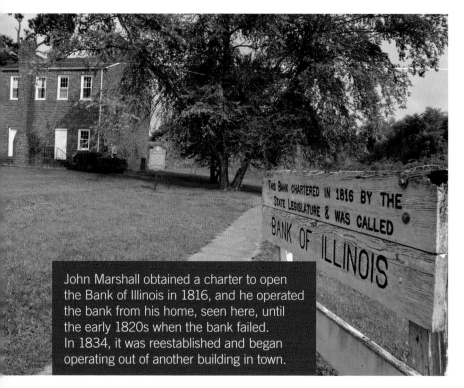

John Marshall obtained a charter to open the Bank of Illinois in 1816, and he operated the bank from his home, seen here, until the early 1820s when the bank failed. In 1834, it was reestablished and began operating out of another building in town.

In the early 1800s, steamboats belching coal smoke and the shouts of thousands dominated the docks at the Ohio River port of Shawneetown Illinois. Surveyed in 1810, Shawneetown had about 40 log structures early on. In addition to being a busy port of call for Ohio River steamships, it was also a salt-mining center and the it was also a salt-mining center and the Gallatin County seat.

Due to its riverbank location, however, it was constantly subjected to the whims of the temperamental Ohio. Citizens often had the "pleasure" and added excitement of river water flowing down the streets and into their businesses and homes. In 1937, after decades of off-and-on flooding, the citizens asked for the assistance of the federal government's Works Progress Administration to relocate the town to higher ground.

Thus, Shawneetown was left to the elements and to whomever might want to brave Old Man River and his mercurial moods. The town was reestablished three miles west, with the original site now becoming known as Old Shawneetown. Most of the city's businesses and the Gallatin County seat relocated, making the Shawneetown home to 1,054 people in 2021.

In late January 1937, unprecedented flooding along the Ohio River washed away towns, killed 385 people, left more than a million people homeless, and caused about half a billion dollars in property damage between Pittsburgh, Pennsylvania, and Cairo, Illinois, which is located at the confluence of the Ohio and the Mississippi rivers. Shawneetown sustained tremendous damage (bottom) and the federal government set up massive tent cities nearby to house the refugees until they could build or relocate (top). As a result of this flood, the physical town of Shawneetown moved to higher ground.

**ABOVE** Built between 1839 and 1841, this Greek Revival bank building was constructed of brick and had a limestone front. The Bank of Illinois opened for business in the new structure in 1841 but closed down in 1843. The building remained vacant until 1854, and since that time, it has been home to various banks until it closed for the last time in 1942. It has been vacant since.

# Victoria, Michigan

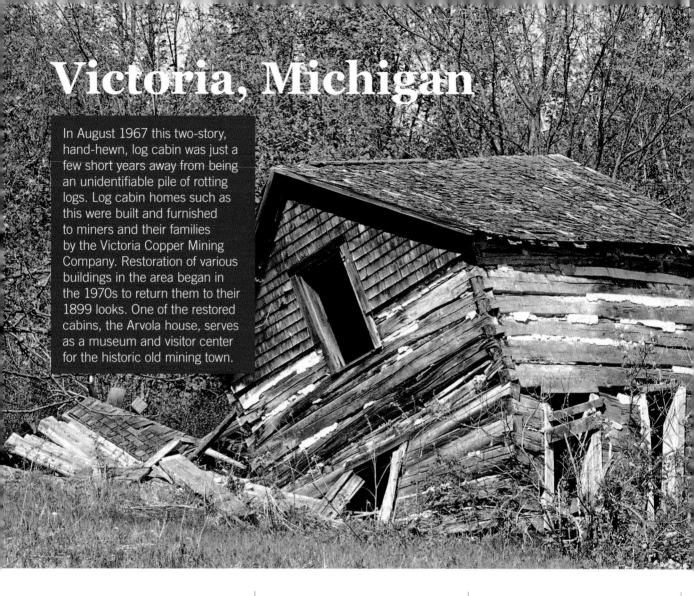

In August 1967 this two-story, hand-hewn, log cabin was just a few short years away from being an unidentifiable pile of rotting logs. Log cabin homes such as this were built and furnished to miners and their families by the Victoria Copper Mining Company. Restoration of various buildings in the area began in the 1970s to return them to their 1899 looks. One of the restored cabins, the Arvola house, serves as a museum and visitor center for the historic old mining town.

Ancient copper mines are said to have excavated tons of workable native copper from Michigan's Upper Peninsula thousands of years ago, leaving no clues as to who they were or where they went. Just before the American Revolution, Alexander Henry came to the area and made an unsuccessful attempt to mine the rich copper that was so pure it could be used raw from the ground.

It wasn't until 1846, however, that a successful attempt was made to extract that copper, and even then, only minor mining occurred until 1899. That was when the boom at the copper mining camp named after

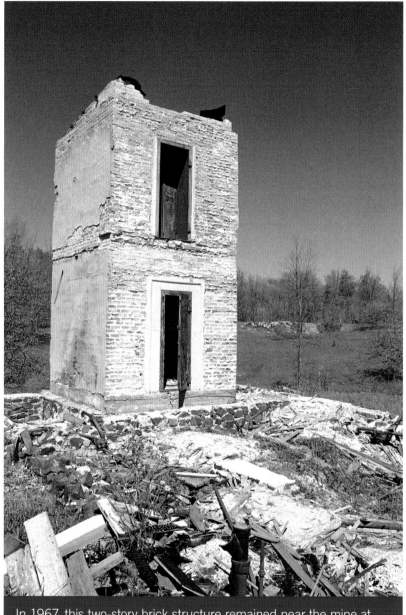

In 1967, this two-story brick structure remained near the mine at the old copper mining town. By the mid-1960s, Victoria was almost gone. Forty years of neglect coupled with the brutal winters of the Upper Peninsula had taken their toll.

England's Queen Victoria began. Miners flocked to the area from all over Europe, including pioneers from Cornwall, Croatia, and Finland.

Victoria was a company mining town financed with English money. The Victoria Mining Company provided 80 cabins, a post office (which opened on September 16, 1899), a general store, and bunkhouses for single miners. Also present were a doctor, a saloon, and a sawmill. Four hundred people lived here in 1905, a number that increased to 750 in 1919.

But when the Victoria mine closed in 1921, the town followed suit, except for the post office, which remained open until December 14, 1935, to serve outlying areas.

**LEFT** To date, four buildings at Victoria have been restored and furnished: the Arvola and the Alexander homes, a boarding house, and the Usimaki house for single miners. The restoration of Victoria is so authentic to the time period that it's almost possible to hear the sounds of children playing on the rope swing hanging from the big tree in front of this cabin . Not only have the cabins in Victoria been restored structurally, they have been furnished accurately to reflect various time periods in the life of the mining camp.

**BELOW** The portion of the 1899 Arvola home apart from the visitor center is authentic right down to the wood-burning stove, utensils, and rat trap. The Alexander home is furnished in a style that was popular when the camp shut down.

This old wooden pipe wrapped in wire once supplied compressed air to the mine from the water-powered, hydraulic compressor plant located near the local dam.

# THE NORTHEASTERN STATES

Stone, mortar, and locally supplied lumber were used to build solid, substantial buildings. Importing construction materials long distances was nearly unheard of and was extremely expensive, besides. Streams and rivers, then, were utilized to supply water and transportation and to power industry, such as this grist mill anchoring the small town of Batsto, New Jersey.

**Of all the regions of the United States, the Northeast is the most difficult in which to find ghost towns. Four hundred years of continual settlement has taken its toll. Land has been claimed, reclaimed, and reclaimed again. Forests have been felled. Communities have sprouted, died, and been plowed over for farming. The fields have been abandoned, forests have returned, and the cycle has continued.**

Milling and textile manufacturing towns were established along rivers where small dams were built, impounding water to power the factories and mills. But shifting economies closed the industries, dams were removed, supporting towns died, and the sites were reclaimed by nature.

Logging camps, mining towns (yes, mining towns), and a plethora of other types of communities have grown, died, and been forgotten over the passage of nearly four centuries of history.

## A Variety of Reasons for Ghost Towns

What these states lack in

Prosperity, especially among mining and other single-economy towns, was often fleeting. When the economic base was producing, boom times prevailed. Rows of stores competed for business, and towns took pride in their commercial districts. However, once that economic base crumbled, the boom burst and people left, abandoning towns such as Centralia, Pennsylvania, to wither and die, their stores vacated and forgotten and their dreams shattered.

ghost-town quantity, they make up for in diversity and age. Some of the oldest ghost towns in the country are located here, mainly because, obviously, this was one of the first regions settled by European colonists. This area was also the focus of the American Revolution and the heart of the Second Industrial Revolution. From the War of 1812 until just after the Civil War, the United States of America made use of its great stockpiles of natural resources, its inventiveness, and its desire for self-sufficiency. The previously agrarian American society was transformed into a major urban industrial powerhouse, a change that was focused in the Northeast.

The mid-1800s were a time of massive migration from Europe to the

**ABOVE** Fire burning below ground, along with mine subsidence in Centralia, Pennsylvania, has buckled State Highway 61. Gaping fissures—some of which can belch toxic smoke—give the old highway an otherworldly, apocalyptic look. The fissured section of the highway south of town has been closed, and a bypass has been built around the problem area.

**BELOW** The ruins of the former anthracite furnace in Hopewell Furnace, Pennsylvania, which was built in 1849.

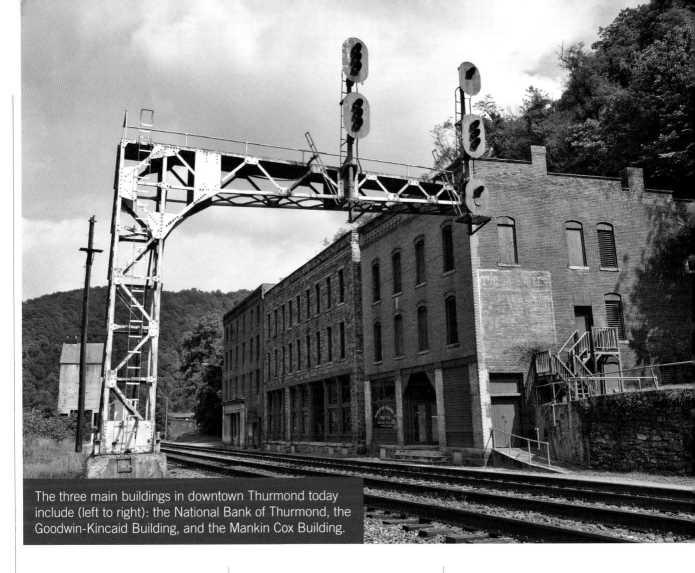

The three main buildings in downtown Thurmond today include (left to right): the National Bank of Thurmond, the Goodwin-Kincaid Building, and the Mankin Cox Building.

rapidly expanding and strengthening America. Immigrants found ready work in the developing American industrial economy. And more people created the need for more goods and services. Iron forges and furnaces, for instance, increased with the demand for iron and steel products, and coal mining surged to fuel the flames of the furnaces. In the early and mid-1800s, railroads extended their steel tentacles throughout the region. Because coal was needed to power the boilers driving the locomotives, even more coal mining and iron furnaces developed. Those two industries created a previously unknown type of community called a company town—a town that is wholly owned, operated, and controlled by the company that owns the industry supporting the community. That type of control, however, also placed each town at greater risk of ghosthood should the company fail or the economy falter.

In addition to the growth, death, and recycling of land and towns, some of America's oldest cities continue to thrive in this region. New York, established in 1624; Boston, in 1630; Providence, 1636; Philadelphia, 1681; and Baltimore, 1729, are all prosperous cities. There are also hundreds of smaller cities and towns that predate the American Revolution. But, despite the urban nature of the region, forests and mountains cover a large percentage of the area away from the coastal plains. And this is where most of the physical remains of ghost towns lie.

## A Different Kind of Ghost Town

Big, brawny Western-style ghost towns do not exist here. Heartland-style faded farm towns filled with complete but abandoned buildings don't exist here, either. Even dead towns filled with roofless building shells aren't found here. What do exist are mostly unidentifiable foundation outlines, cellar holes, and the broken stubs of rock walls hidden in the trees. In a few locations, specific ghost towns have been restored to show visitors what life was like in the pioneering days. Some of these include Batsto, New Jersey, and Hopewell Furnace, Pennsylvania. The ebb and flow of civilization in this small, densely populated region have played havoc on tangible remains. Yet some things do remain; it just takes research and shoe leather to discover them.

Deep in the forests of Pennsylvania and West Virginia, coal-mining towns and iron-furnace towns remain. Some have been forgotten, and some have been restored. Faded agricultural towns and fishing villages that flirt with ghosthood line the Piedmont and coastal plains on the eastern side of the Appalachian Mountains. The Pine Barrens of New Jersey support a large number of bog-iron communities, some completely lost and forgotten, some

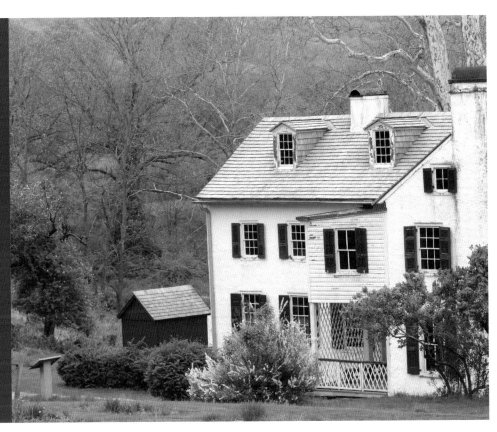

As European settlement advanced into the wilderness, small communities were established to service travelers, support logging or mining towns, or act as harbingers of a commercial boom in a new location. When industrial towns such as iron furnace communities were established, they were often company owned; the company manager would build large homes, such as this one in Hopewell Furnace, Pennsylvania, to accommodate their comfort.

restored. New England has missing mill towns, lost logging camps, forgotten fishing villages, and other communities, now known only to the vapors of the past.

The Northeast was America's front door. Millions of immigrants touched the soil of their new home at crowded immigration stations in New York and Baltimore. Military posts and forts bristled with cannons and massive brick walls, ready to repel any and all invaders. Lighthouses and their tiny self-contained communities dotted sandy and rocky headlands alike, warning ships of danger.

If visits are timed correctly, the curious can have the deserted but restored streets to themselves. Here in History Central, the sounds of ghost commerce, ghost industrialization, and ghost life can still be found.

# Centralia, Pennsylvania

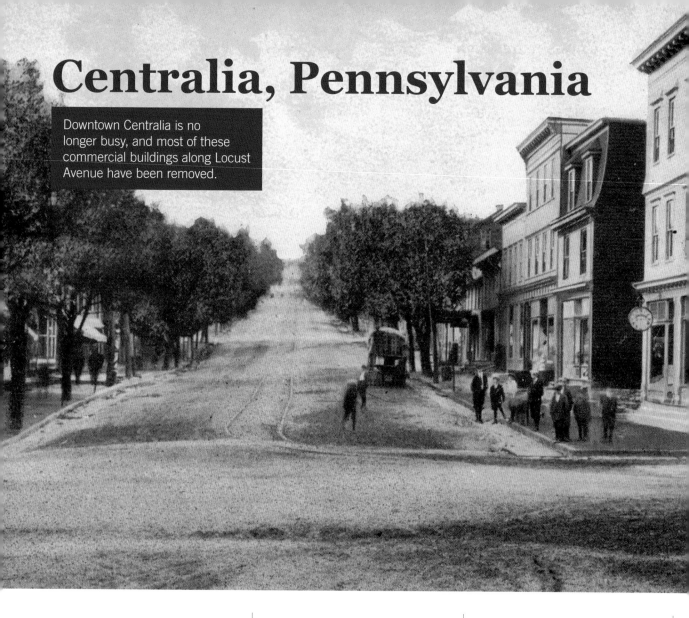

Downtown Centralia is no longer busy, and most of these commercial buildings along Locust Avenue have been removed.

Centralia started out as a typical nondescript northeastern Pennsylvania coal-mining town. Established in 1854 as Centreville, it was renamed Centralia when the post office refused the original name. In 1866 it incorporated as a borough, and for the next hundred years or so it was a bustling anthracite coal–mining town with its population wave following the fortunes of the coal industry. In 1930 there were 2,446 people; in 1980 there were 1,017; and in 2008 only 20 residents still lived there. Since 1984,

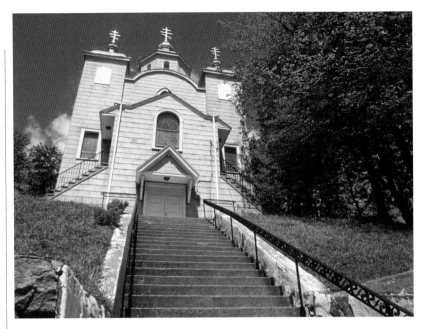

**ABOVE** Saints Peter and Paul Ukrainian Catholic Church and its adjacent cemetery were located on the hill overlooking Centralia. The church closed as a result of the mine fire in 1985.

**BELOW** In the foreground of this photo is one of more than 1,000 vents drilled to allow toxic gases and smoke produced by the underground fire to escape. In the background are a few of Centralia's remaining homes.

there has been a mass exodus as the federal and state governments have been booting folks out.

It was all because of the burning dump, which was, unfortunately, located in an abandoned mine pit next to the Independent Order of Odd Fellows Cemetery. On May 27, 1962, the Borough's Fire Department decided to burn trash to rid the area of its "dump smell" for the upcoming Memorial Day Weekend. A nice gesture, but . . .

When the fire burned down to the bottom of the trash layer, it entered an unsealed opening that reached back into the honeycomb of century-old coal-mine tunnels. Poof! The seam of underground coal caught fire. Today, that fire continues to burn under Centralia and its last few holdouts.

# Hopewell Furnace, Pennsylvania

The restored casting shed complex included a large building that sheltered casting operations from the weather. Inside were furnaces and sandcasting beds, where pig iron was cast into ingots. Stoves and other cast-iron products were manufactured in another part of the building.

H opewell Furnace dates to 1771, when the hardwood charcoal-powered furnace was built to take advantage of iron deposits ten miles south of iron industrialist Mark Bird's existing Hopewell Forge. Bird relocated his Hopewell operations to the new site, building a supporting village around them.

In 1772, the furnace produced pots, stove plates, tools, and window-sash weights, as well as cannons and shot for the Continental Army and Navy.

After the Revolutionary War ended, Bird sold the Hopewell furnace, but in 1816, it again produced iron products. Within ten years, production reached about 700 tons a year. The supporting village of Hopewell Furnace had roughly 1,000 people

**LEFT** The Ironmaster's Mansion housed the ironmaster and his family. There were also accommodations for the servants and guests. On the second floor, a study also served as a library and sitting room and was where numerous business transactions occurred. Between 1800 and 1828, the building was constructed in three different phases.

and included businesses and institutions such as a company store, a blacksmith, a livery stable/barn, a wheelwright, the ironmaster's mansion, homes for workers, a church, and a schoolhouse.

Unfortunately for this community, the end for the inefficient charcoal-powered furnaces came around 1850. Production decreased until a flurry of activity occurred during the Civil War, but it slowed again afterward. The fires finally flickered out for good in 1883.

Four of Hopewell Furnace's 14 restored buildings are shown here. The store, dating to 1784, is on the left. It was a "company store" in that all the needs of the iron plantation workers could be purchased here on credit against their wages. In the center background is the ironmaster's 14-room mansion, which was also known as the "Big House."

# Batsto, New Jersey

The 32-room ironmaster's mansion marks the heart of Batsto. It was originally built for the ironmaster and his family, but after Batsto faded, Joseph Wharton used it to oversee his large estate. Portions of this magnificent home are open for tours.

Charles Read established a charcoal-powered iron forge and village in 1766 to tap the abundant bog iron resources in the Batsto River, as well as in other nearby streams and swamps. In 1773 he sold out to John Cox of Philadelphia, who took over the operation and produced skillets, kettles, pots, and all sorts of household goods. During the Revolutionary War, Batsto's furnaces also produced cannonballs. After the war and its massive need for iron products ended, other industries such as brickyards, glassworks, a gristmill, and a sawmill also operated here, keeping the village active and growing upward in population to about 1,000.

**ABOVE** This mill was built by Joseph Wharton to replace a previous one that dated back to the early days of Batsto. Wharton sold lumber and wooden shingles all over the region, which proved to be a profitable business venture for him. The mill is still usable.

**BELOW** Horses and mules were used in the operations here, and they were housed in this restored stone barn, which was built in 1828. Hay was stored above the stalls.

But like charcoal-powered iron forges elsewhere, the furnaces at Batsto couldn't compete with coal-powered operations. By 1848, they had shut down. The town itself hung in there until 1874 when a fire decimated half of its buildings.

In 1876, Joseph Wharton purchased the property—he farmed the region and operated the sawmill. Finally, in 1954, the state of New Jersey, recognizing the historical aspect of the property, purchased it and established the Wharton State Forest and Batsto State Historic Site. About 40 buildings in the old town have been restored. Today, Batsto is a monument to the perseverance and tenacity of the early ironworkers in America's hinterlands.

# Thurmond, West Virginia

A recent view of the railroad station, which was restored in 1995 by the National Park Service. It now serves as Thurmond's visitor center.

Imagine a bustling railroad town populated by 500 people and filled with multistory wood, brick, and rock buildings housing banks, stores, and large hotels. Imagine a railroad depot serving 75,000 passengers a year. Imagine all this without a main street!

Thurmond was founded in the 1880s along the Chesapeake and Ohio (C&O) Railway. Due to the narrow riverside bench on which the town sat, there was no room for a traditional main street in addition to the railroad. The buildings were all built fronting the town's economic lifeline, with just a narrow walkway between the iron rails and the front doors.

From the 1890s to 1930, Thurmond boomed. In 1930, 482 people lived here, but bust quickly supplanted boom when the massive Dunglen Hotel burned in 1930, followed by failure of the National Bank of Thurmond. As rail traffic slowed, businesses failed. After World War II,

Still standing, this concrete coaling tower was built in 1922 to load coal into the tenders of the C&O steam trains. The trains pulled beneath the tower or on the two sides, where chutes were lowered to load the tenders. By 1960, the coal-fired steam engines were gone, and the 500-ton capacity tower was abandoned.

railroads switched from coal- to diesel-powered locomotives. Train trips through Thurmond and the gorge decreased, along with the lessened demand for coal. Ultimately, diesel engines became the death of Thurmond's steam engine repair yards, coaling stations, and water tanks. Over the years, fires turned landmarks into memories.

The downtown core, restored railroad depot, church, and a couple dozen homes housing the town's seven people still remain, a classic link to the past.

**RIGHT** In November 1988 the former engine house and sand tower of the Chesapeake & Ohio Railway at Thurmond were still standing. The C&O employed hundreds of workers at its Thurmond yards in the early 1900s. The engine house was built around 1902 and expanded about 100 feet in 1921. The large building burned in 1993.

HAER No WV-43-4

# THE SOUTHEASTERN STATES

Between 1858 and 1860, Joseph Babcock built a 15,000-square-foot brick warehouse/cotton shed on top of an old Native American mound above the Alabama River. When the Civil War came to Cahawba, a stockade was built around the building and the property was used to house prisoners of war, holding as many as 3,000 Union soldiers.

**The state of Florida has the distinction of being the home to America's oldest ghost town site as well its oldest continuously occupied city. The original Spanish colony of Pensacola was established in 1559, but just a few months after that, it was wiped out by a hurricane; two years later it was finally abandoned. In 1565, St. Augustine, America's oldest continuously occupied city, was founded.**

The second oldest town site is Charlesfort, South

Whether a particular incident occurred in an entire town or in a single building like this one—the McLean Mansion in Appomattox Court House, Virginia, where the Civil War officially ended—that event becomes synonymous with that structure or location. That one instant in time becomes the focus, while the years, decades, or centuries before and after become lost to the recesses of history. Before and after become irrelevant, forgotten, or both.

Carolina, located on present-day Parris Island. It was established by the French in 1562 and abandoned the next year. Three years after that, the Spanish founded Santa Elena, a colony and fort at the old French site, which they occupied for more than 20 years until 1587.

The first English colony was Fort Raleigh, North Carolina, which dates to 1584. It failed, but mystery has surrounded that fate ever since. Twenty-three years later, in 1607, the first successful British colony was located at Jamestown, Virginia.

## The Scramble for Riches

America's first documented gold mine is also located in the South. The Reed

Mine was discovered in southwestern North Carolina in 1799, creating a limited rush into the area. For the next 30 years, this region was the nation's leading producer of that precious metal, and some 30,000 people have been estimated to have worked those gold fields. In 1828 that all ended with the discovery of gold in the Dahlonega, Georgia, area. Gold fever spread southwest toward northern Alabama and then back up into the Piedmont region of North Carolina and Virginia. In 1848, however, the door slammed shut on Southern gold mines when news of the California Gold Rush electrified the nation.

Many crossroads taverns, also called ordinaries, were established along southern pikes, or highways. These travel stops served food and beverages of choice and offered lodging for travelers. Often additional businesses such as general stores, blacksmiths, and liveries established themselves adjacent to the inns, creating the nucleus for a small town. When the country roads were paved and automobiles replaced horses as the main transportation, many of these locations faded and died, especially those located off the main travel routes.

Ghost towns were also created by old ferry crossings, as the Southeast is blessed with many rivers—even if the river crossings were quite often problematic. Enterprising folks established ferries at key locations where busy roads crossed the water, and these spots often came to include an inn or other

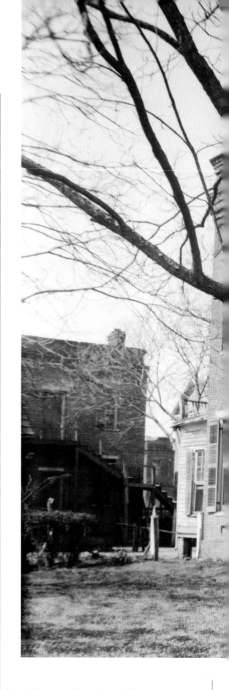

business designed to serve travelers. Together, these would be the core of another town. When ferries began

Boom, then bust. Boom, then bust. On and on and on. Since the 18th century, this has been the life cycle for thousands of towns across the region. The town's citizens might live a hard-scrabble life, but a select few, due to fortunate circumstances or title, had money. Their prosperity would be shown to all by the construction of great homes, such as the Kirkpatrick Mansion of Cahawba, Alabama. Yet the life cycles of towns ate up the rich as well as the poor, and often these old mansions were vacated when the rest of the towns failed.

to be replaced by bridges or were washed away, or when the roads relocated, another ghost town was born.

## Left Over From Plantation Culture

Larger sugar and cotton plantations have generally been unknown sources of ghost towns. Small villages were often established in or around the plantations, creating self-supporting communities that housed the workers, either free or slave. The sugar plantations specialized in raising sugarcane, which was rendered into molasses. Since sugarcane is a tropical plant, most such plantations were located in Louisiana or Florida.

After the cotton gin was invented in 1792, cotton became the most lucrative agricultural product in the South, with yields increasing steadily until 1860, at which time the South is said to have produced two-thirds of the world's cotton supply. Like sugar, much of that cotton was produced on huge

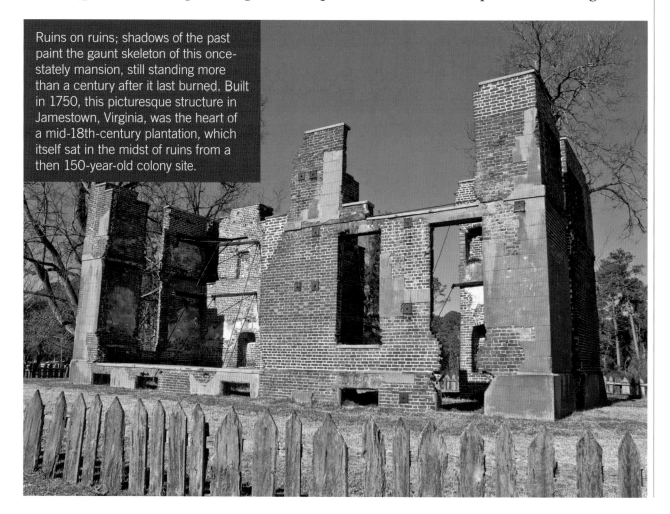

Ruins on ruins; shadows of the past paint the gaunt skeleton of this once-stately mansion, still standing more than a century after it last burned. Built in 1750, this picturesque structure in Jamestown, Virginia, was the heart of a mid-18th-century plantation, which itself sat in the midst of ruins from a then 150-year-old colony site.

estates or plantations that were self-contained communities. The rest was grown on smaller farms. But the Civil War changed all that.

After the war ended, slavery was abolished and plantation culture ultimately died, having been replaced by smaller family farms or sharecroppers. Centrally located market and milling towns supported these farms, but even these began to fade out by the 1950s. The biggest cotton producing states were Alabama, Mississippi, and South Carolina.

## Other Causes of Ghost Towns

Coal mining in the Appalachian Mountains of Kentucky and Tennessee, as well as on the outer fringes of several other states, began in the early 1800s and continued unabated until the late 1930s. This industry began to fade after the end of World War II, when oil became the energy source of choice and the declining demand for coal killed off hundreds, if not thousands, of Appalachian coal-mining towns. Today, coal is still extensively mined, but company-owned coal-mining camps have slipped into the past.

Then there is the Tennessee Valley Authority. Beginning in the mid-1930s as part of Franklin Roosevelt's New Deal, the TVA built dozens of hydro-electric dams along the Tennessee River system in the western Appalachian region. These massive reservoirs tamed once-wild rivers, but in the process many towns had to be vacated, razed, or relocated. Their old sites are now underwater, mere memories and names on pre-1930s era maps.

Throughout Alabama, Kentucky, Tennessee, and Virginia, iron furnaces developed as early as the 1600s. They really came into their own by the early 1800s with the advent of the American Industrial Revolution. Each of these furnaces supported small self-sufficient towns lasting until most of the furnaces shut down during the Civil War. A few furnaces managed to reopen, but the war pretty much put an end to this kind of small independent operator. Dixie is filled with ghost towns, many of which have long since become nothing but shadows of the past.

# Appomattox Courthouse, Virginia

Around 1819, the Clover Hill Tavern (right) was established along the Richmond-Lynchburg Stage Coach Road. It served as a way station for travelers, who could obtain food, drink, and overnight accommodations here. In 1845, Appomattox County was formed, and the tiny hamlet of Clover Hill obtained the county seat honors. A new courthouse (left) was built in 1846 and served as the seat of government until it burned in 1892. At that time, the county seat was shifted three miles to the town of Appomattox, and Appomattox Court House languished in its Civil War fame. The courthouse building was reconstructed in 1964.

**M**anassas Junction, Virginia. July 21, 1861. Retired Army Major Wilmer McLean and his wife Virginia loaned their home to Confederate Brigadier General P.G.T. Beauregard for his headquarters while he planned the first major assault against Union forces gathering nearby. Union cannonballs pummeled the house, and the Civil War's first major battle was underway.

In 1863, the McLeans headed south to another quiet little Virginia town.

One evening—Palm Sunday, April 9, 1865—Wilmer McLean heard a knock at the door. There stood Confederate General Robert E. Lee, who was ushered into the parlor. A half hour later, General Ulysses S. Grant entered the home and was also ushered into the parlor.

**ABOVE** In addition to the main tavern building, the Clover Hill Tavern also had a freestanding guesthouse located on the property. Built at the same time as the main tavern in 1819, this three-story brick structure was graced with exterior balconies and stairs, allowing each room private access.

**LEFT** This log outbuilding at the McLean house served as slave quarters during the years the McLean home served as a tavern.

Appomattox Court House, the tiny, nondescript 20-year-old county seat for Appomattox County, Virginia, with its brick courthouse and handful of other buildings, dozed quietly that Sunday afternoon, its place in American history just having been secured.

A week earlier, the Civil War was closing in on the sleepy Piedmont town with its two blacksmith shops, county jail, law offices, two stables, three stores, a tavern, and homes for 150 or so people. General Lee's Army of Northern Virginia was being dogged by General Grant's boys in blue.

Poor old Wilber McLean. His home at Manassas Junction saw the first major battle of the Civil War. Four years later, the parlor of his home at Appomattox Court House saw the formal end of the war.

# Jamestown, Virginia

After a four and a half month transatlantic crossing, then two weeks of exploring the coastline for a suitable colony site, three ragtag English ships carrying 104 men and boys landed along the marshy north bank of what would be named the James River in the future colony and state of Virginia. It was May 13, 1607, and the first successful English colony in the New World was about to be established.

The settlers quickly erected a triangular, wood-walled fort and filled it in with English-style buildings constructed of saplings and mud, with thatched roofing. Some of the structures included communal buildings, a church, homes, and storehouses. Life here

Today's Jamestown exists in two parts. The original site, called "Historic Jamestowne," is part of Colonial National Historic Park. Abutting it on the west is "Jamestown Settlement," a living history museum administered by the state of Virginia and consisting of reconstructions of both Jamestown and a Powhatan village populated by period-costumed docents. The thatch-roofed, straw-mud walled buildings have been accurately recreated.

**ABOVE** Today actors recreate everyday life of the settlers for visitros at the Colonial National Historic Park.

**BELOW** The weathered brick ruin of Jamestown's church tower is the only original structure remaining above ground at the original colony site. This tower is all that is left of the brick church built in 1676 to replace a series of churches on the same site, the last of which had been burned during Bacon's Rebellion that year. The 1676 church was used until about 1750, when it was abandoned. In 1893, the Association for the Preservation of Virginia Antiquities obtained the property and preserved the tower in its 1893 condition.

was no Garden of Eden. The colonists set out gardens, hunted, traded with the local Native Americans, drank bad water, fought mosquitoes, and tried to build a stable life. Despite the arrival of fresh batches of colonists, by the end of 1610, the population had dwindled to 60.

From the summer of 1610 on, however, enough new settlers arrived and new crops were tried that the original investment began to pay off, and the colony expanded. In 1624, the original charter issued to the private Virginia Company was revoked by King James I. He turned Jamestown and Virginia into an English Crown Colony. After 91 years of being at Jamestown, the Virginia colonial capital was switched to the nearby settlement of Williamsburg in 1699. Jamestownwas abandoned.

# Barthell and Blue Heron, Kentucky

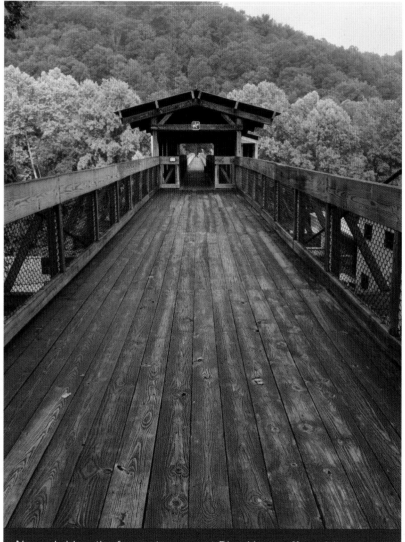

Now a bridge, the former tramway at Blue Heron offers visitors a bird's-eye view of the ghost coal camp. Established by the Michigan-based Stearns Coal and Lumber company, Blue Heron was a typical mid-20th-century company town.

During the early 1900s, the Stearns Coal & Lumber Company operated a number of mines and mining camps from their headquarters at Stearns, Kentucky. Mines #1 and #2 supported the camp of Barthell, while Mine #18 supported the small camp of Blue Heron.

The Stearns Mines #1 and #2 at Barthell began operation in 1903, and the camp was built at that time. A little "disagreement" over union or nonunion mining resulted in the hotel being burned in 1908.

Up through the 1930s, Barthell had at least 200 miners and a number of buildings, including a company store,

This coal tipple at Blue Heron has been reconstructed. The term tipple originally applied to an elevated area where coal cars coming out of a mine were tipped to empty their coal into large bins, but the definition now includes large structures that do that same thing and more. Most of these tipples incorporate conveyor systems and other unloading methods in addition to tipping the mine cars.

**ABOVE** Barthell was established in 1902, Stearns Coal and Lumber Company's first mine and mining camp in the area. It quickly developed into a bustling town along Roaring Paunch Creek. This photograph was taken sometime after the Kentucky & Tennessee Railroad arrived in the booming coal camp in 1903.

a post office, a railroad depot, a combined church and school, a doctor's office, a barbershop, and a bathhouse. In 1943, Mine #1 closed after the coal-loading plant and neighboring buildings burned and weren't replaced. In 1953, Mine #2 closed, and in 1959, the last person left town. A number of Barthell's buildings have

been reconstructed to the original plans.

Blue Heron is located southwest of Barthell and once had 300 miners. Mine #18 and the camp that accompanied it operated from 1937 through December 1962. Blue Heron was a small camp, the last owned and operated by the Stearns Company. It

consisted of a company store, a railroad depot, a church, a school, a bathhouse, and homes. During the 1980s, a number of these buildings were rebuilt as empty shells on display to show what the buildings looked like but lacking the "guts." Inside each of these structures, the National Park Service shares the history of life in the old coal-mining camp.

# Cahawba, Alabama

This colonnaded home was built by Samuel and Sarah Kirkpatrick during Cahawba's second boom, which started in 1858 with the promise of a railroad. The railroad came the next year and ushered in prosperity. People flocked to the booming town, and numerous successful individuals and families constructed large homes and mansions. Life was good—until the Civil War started.

Southwest of Selma, Alabama, at the confluence of Cahaba and Alabama rivers, is the old town site of Cahawba (also spelled Cahaba). Like a cat, this old town has led multiple lives. It began as the first permanent state capital for the state of Alabama and was also the designated county seat for Dallas County.

In the 1820s, a combination of yellow fever and flooding spelled trouble for Cahawba. By just one vote in 1825, the state capital was relocated to Tuscaloosa. Cahawba stumbled but didn't fall.

The resilient citizens saw a bright future as a major river port. Word got out, and new residents kept coming. Rebuilding continued unabated. In 1859, the railroad came through, and some 3,000 people called Cahawba home.

But then the Civil War came to Alabama. Cahawba's railroad was torn up, and a 3,000-person POW camp for captured Union soldiers was established. Nearby Selma was sacked and burned, but Cahawba was spared that indignity when another flood swept through before the Union troops could. But by war's end, Cahawba was nonetheless crippled. Adding insult to injury, the county seat was relocated to a rebuilt Selma in 1866. Reality hit hard. Cahawba was doomed.

During Reconstruction, a nearly abandoned Cahawba revived—somewhat. Former slaves came, turning the town site into an agricultural community filled with family farms. Unfortunately, however, that didn't last. By 1900, the abandoned ruins were becoming one with nature, and by the 1930s little remained.

**LEFT** This cabin is not one of Cahawba's older structures, dating only into the early 20th century. It provided a home for some of Cahawba's later citizenry.

# Auraria, Georgia

In 1900 the Castleberry family of Auraria posed in this wagon pulled by an ox.

**T**he ghost of Auraria hides in the wrinkled corduroy piedmont at the southern end of the Appalachian Mountains in northern Georgia, about seven miles southwest of Dahlonega and 60 miles north of Atlanta. Today's Auraria is nothing like 1830s Auraria, when the booming gold-mining town had a weekly newspaper, as well as enough saloons, hotels, and other businesses to supply the needs of 1,000 miners and other camp hangers-on.

Gold was discovered here around 1828, igniting the

**ABOVE** This red cabin is said to have been the homestead for Emory Brackett. Some call it Auraria's bank, but it appears that the bank was elsewhere. Another uncertainty is the naming of the town. According to the on-site historical monument, Auraria was named by U.S. Vice President John C. Calhoun, who also owned one of the earliest and richest gold mines to the east of town. Others, however, claim local citizen Major John Powell named the town.

**BELOW** Scattered about the area are numerous old cabins and homes dating back to the 19th century.

Georgia Gold Rush the following year. For the next 20 years, this region was the place to be, an area where towns popped up like mushrooms on a wet lawn. Auraria boomed quickly, challenging Dahlonega for the county seat. Dahlonega won and grew, and Auraria slowly faded through the 1830s and was almost completely depopulated when news of the California Gold Rush reached the mines of Georgia in 1848.

Having lost its will to live, with the farming capabilities in the area being recognized as poor and with few miners remaining, Auraria turned up its boots, laid down, and died. Today, the old Woody's Store building, Graham Hotel, and a few homes are all that remain. Those and memories of the days of old, days of gold, days of '29!

# Bullowville, Florida

Built on coquina shell limestone, these rock ruins are all that remain of the former sugar mill at Bulowville. Charles Bulow established the plantation and built the sugar plant. After he died in 1823, his son, John, came home from Paris, France, to take over the family business. The mill thrived, and so did John Bulow. He had befriended the Seminole, becoming an outspoken critic of the government's relocation plan for them. In 1836, a small state militia marched on Bulowville, and Bulow fired an empty cannon at the soldiers. They captured Bulow and the plantation, using it for forays against the Seminole.

Florida is an unlikely state in which to find ghost towns. At least, that's the popular misconception. In the Sunshine State, there are more than 300 of these old places hidden in the greenery, lost in the outback, or paved over, their sites bristling with tourist traps, mini malls, and subdivisions.

Bulowville is the ruin of an old sugar plantation "village" plopped along the upper east coast of Florida, just shy of 20 miles north of Daytona Beach. It is tucked under the trees at the north end of Bulow Creek State Park, on the south side of a mobile home park. Ruins remain of the plantation owner's mansion, well, boat docks, spring house, and sugar mill, as well as of coquina shell limestone foundations for some of the 46 12-foot by 16-foot slave houses.

Charles W. Bulow and his son John established this plantation, the largest sugar mill in Florida, in 1821. They cleared the land, planted the sugarcane in January and February, and harvested the crop in late October. Some 150 to 300 slave workers cut the cane, loaded it onto carts, and hauled it to the mill where it was rendered. Cotton, indigo, and rice were also raised in this self-sufficient little village.

In January 1836, during the 2nd Seminole War, the Seminole burned 16 plantations, including this one. It was never rebuilt, and today the ruins are a state historic park.

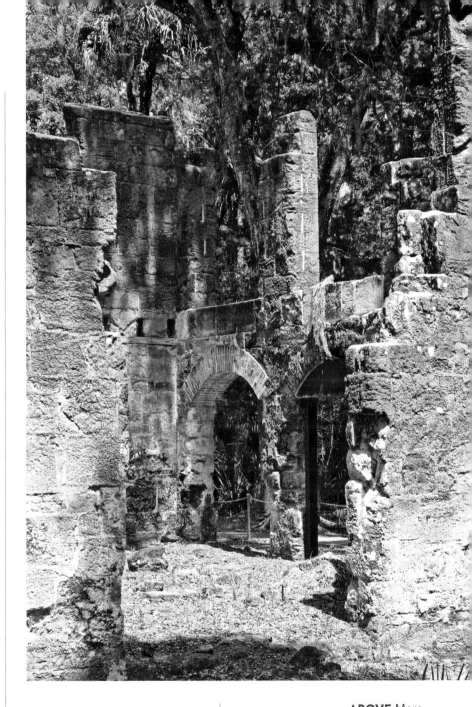

**ABOVE** More foundational remnants built from the coquina shell limtestone.

# HAWAII, ALASKA, AND WESTERN CANADA

A photo of Dawson City nestled along the Yukon River in 1898.

**These may be three seemingly unrelated areas, but one similarity they share is that they are ripe with ghost towns, including one of the most unique ghost towns in the world.**

## The Great Pacific

Hawaii is one of America's prime vacation spots, but very few of the visitors there know about the 50th state's ghost towns. Beginning in the mid-1800s and continuing through the 1900s, the sugar industry gave rise to company-owned towns supporting plantations and mills on the islands. Some of these mills operated until the early 2000s, although most had previously closed. Sugarcane was first grown commercially in 1835, with the peak years of production running from the 1920s through the early 1990s.

In addition to the company-owned sugar towns, two other creators of ghost towns were environmental—slow, viscous, flowing lava and a tsunami. Over the years, a number of towns on the Big Island of Hawaii have been destroyed by lava flows, including several in 1960 and more again around 1990. Ruins also remain of a number of coastal communities slammed by a tsunami generated by an 8.1-magnitude earthquake at Alaska's Aleutian island of Unimak on April 1, 1946. The 36-foot tsunami that struck the Hawaiian Islands around 7:00 a.m. was one of the most severe to ever strike the islands, causing millions of dollars in damage and killing 159 people in and around Hilo. Some of the seriously damaged coastal towns were never rebuilt. Hawaii also plays host to a pair of unique ghost towns, which were former centers for sufferers of Hansen's disease (for thousands of years known as leprosy).

## The Alaskan Peninsula

North to Alaska, America's last frontier has a huge collection of old mining towns, remnants of the late 19th- and early 20th-century gold rushes that rocked the then territory. Beginning around 1880 at Juneau, prospectors roamed the massive territory for gold, making discoveries at Fortymile in 1886, on the Kenai Peninsula at Hope in 1893, and at Nome in 1898. These early rushes were eclipsed by the discovery of gold in

Canada's Yukon Territory in 1896. Although not in Alaska, this discovery affected the future state, as the main port of entry for the Yukon mines was at the head of the Lynn Canal at the north end of the panhandle. Skagway and Dyea quickly developed into entrances into the backcountry. These two towns are where the 96ers would supply themselves with provisions and begin their brutal 550-mile overland trek up and over Chilkoot Pass and on to Dawson City.

The Alaska-Yukon Gold Rush focused prospectors on Alaska's interior. As mining spread, towns developed, flourished, and then died as the miners moved on. Today many of these old towns are just barely clinging to life. Many of the dead ones are forgotten. Some are accessible, but Alaskan highways are few, and distances are vast.

## The Great White North

America's northern neighbor, Canada, is a huge country. Like the United States, it has thousands of ghost towns stretching coast to coast. The great Alaska-Yukon Gold Rush of 1896 focused the

Sometimes pioneering towns were situated in strategic locations, so once the boom that created them subsided, the towns remained alive, albeit much smaller than during the boom days. Over the years, their century-old buildings have been restored, repainted, and repurposed, as has happened with The Mascot in Skagway, Alaska.

attention of the world on Canada's northwest. Scores of thousands of miners trekked into the rugged region, opening up the vast interior of Alaska and northwestern Canada. Mining towns sprouted and withered, and Dawson City became a household name. This last great gold rush gave the world Sourdoughs, Cheechakos, and Jack London. Even Arizona legend Wyatt Earp ventured up here.

Down in the wide-open plains east of Alberta's Rocky Mountains, coal miners poked holes into the Canadian prairie, giving birth to mining towns that followed the typical cycle, fading in the mid-1900s. Several major clusters of mining towns popped up along the east side

**ABOVE** Alaska is blessed with some of the most beautiful scenery in the world, as well as some of the finest ghost town ruins. Rickety old mining structures such as Independence Mine remain scattered throughout the outback, while the dead supporting towns sit nearby. Because of the brutal Alaskan winters, once these mines closed, the towns died quickly and were often left to the elements. This was a hard life, and very few of these one-economy towns survived once that economic base crumbled.

of the mountains west of Edmonton, west of Calgary. Another large group plopped down in the middle of the Crowsnest Pass area south of Calgary and just north of the U.S./Canada border at Waterton Lakes National Park. In the early 1900s, another cluster of small coal camps popped up in the Drumheller Valley area southeast of Calgary. Most of these old coal camps are now only memories, but quite a few still have viable remains, including the massive Atlas Mine coal tipple.

On the west side of the Rockies, British Columbia has a virtual smorgasbord of ghost towns of many varieties. Here industries such as mining, fishing, the military, and railroads built, nourished, and supported flourishing towns. But the pattern is clear by now: As the industries faded, the towns died.

During the 1860s, gold mining gave rise to numerous mining towns, one of which, Barkerville, is a grand example of the genre. Today, this restored mining town is a provincial park sharing the shining story of the Cariboo Gold Rush. Other mining towns lie throughout the interior, relics of the mid-century Fraser and Peace River rushes.

Along the Pacific Coast, fishing villages and other points of settlement boomed and faded. Fur, agriculture, lumber, and mining gained in importance. As British Columbia gained notoriety, it was added to the expanding nation of Canada as a province in 1871. The military also established a number of forts for protection, some of which became small self-sufficient communities.

Today the relics of Hawaii's company-owned sugar towns draw tourists. Alaska's gold rush heritage is celebrated, and the entire state still reaps the rewards of the great gold rush, as does Canada's Yukon Territory and Dawson City. The former coal camps of Alberta have faded, their bustling streets now deserted, while the old ghosts of British Columbia quietly bask in the glory of days past.

**ABOVE** Skagway's Gold Rush cemetery was the last resting place for many miners who never made it beyond the diversions offered in town. Jefferson Randolph "Soapy" Smith II, a gold rush–era con artist, saloon owner, and ring leader of crime in and around Skagway, is interred here, as is Frank Reid, one of his victims.

**RIGHT** Due to isolation and long travel distances from product markets, old mining towns in the Alaskan backcountry required self-sufficiency. Complete towns were built up around the mines, and huge mills cascaded down the sides of hills, such as the Kennecott Mining Company Mill does here. Built of easily obtainable wood, these massive complexes often towered over the supporting community. Yet size doesn't always matter. Once the ore ran out or became unprofitable to mine, the mine closed, the mill shut down, and the people caught the last train out.

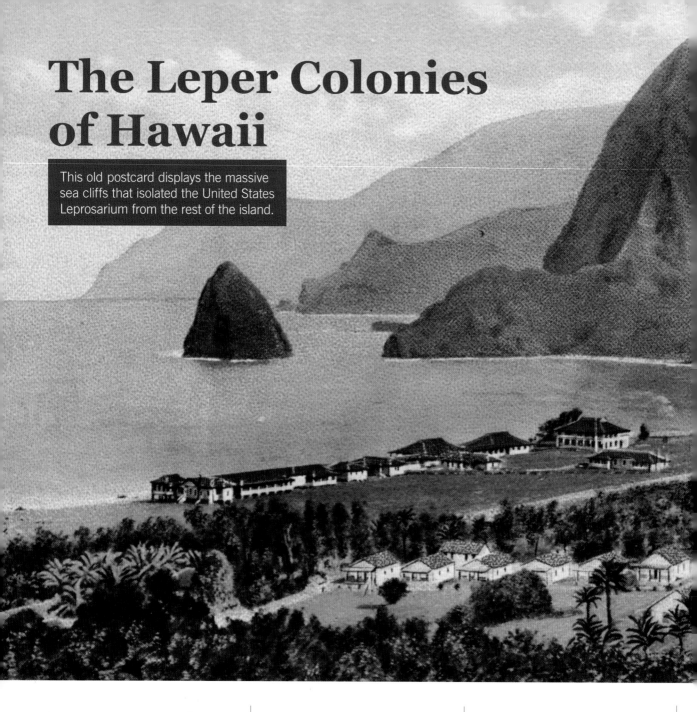

# The Leper Colonies of Hawaii

This old postcard displays the massive sea cliffs that isolated the United States Leprosarium from the rest of the island.

Leprosy, or what is now called Hansen's disease, is controllable by drugs, and is not the scourge it once was. This disease was introduced to the kingdom of Hawaii around 1848. Since there was no known were established to hold those with the disease in isolation. In 1864, 24-year-old Father Damien (born Joseph de Veuster in Belgium) arrived in the Hawaiian Islands as a Catholic missionary. Seven years later, he asked his bishop to be transferred to the leper colonies so he could minister to the afflicted residents there. For 16 years, he provided compassionate care and spiritual guidance for the residents of the two colonies. Then on April 15, 1889, Father Damien died, a victim of that very disease.

In 1980, Kalaupapa and Kalawao became a national historic park due to their importance to both Hawaiian and American history.

treatment at that time, victims of the disease were exiled to the north side of the island of Molokai. In 1866, the Kalaupapa and Kalawao Leper Colonies

**ABOVE** When Belgian-born Catholic priest Father Damien went to the Kalaupapa and Kalawao Leper Colonies willingly, he knew the risks. He spent the rest of his life ministering to the residents. On Sunday, October 11, 2009, Father Damien's work at the colony was recognized when he was canonized by Pope Benedict XVI, who elevated the humble priest to sainthood. Here we see Father Damien with 64 boys who lived in the colony just weeks before his death from succumbing to leprosy in 1889.

**RIGHT** Abandoned homes such as this once housed the former residents of the Kalaupapa community.

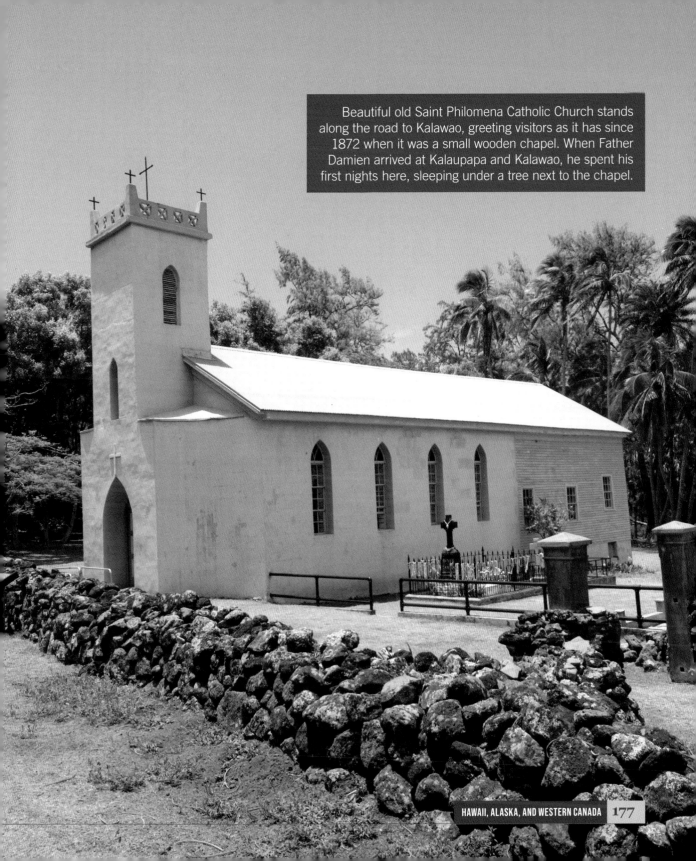

Beautiful old Saint Philomena Catholic Church stands along the road to Kalawao, greeting visitors as it has since 1872 when it was a small wooden chapel. When Father Damien arrived at Kalaupapa and Kalawao, he spent his first nights here, sleeping under a tree next to the chapel.

# Independence Mine, Alaska

This view of the southern portion of the camp shows restored buildings below the ore train tracks and the crumbling mill building. The white buildings from left to right are: an interpretive shelter, which offers site information; the mine office, commissary, and post office building; a four-room apartment built in 1937; and the "new" cookhouse/mess hall built in 1941 with apartments for supervisors on its second floor.

Six million dollars– that's the reported production from the Independence Mine located in Hatcher Pass, about 16 air miles north of Wasilla, Alaska. This mine and its wonderfully picturesque ruins are relics of the mid-20th century.

The original gold in Hatcher Pass was discovered in 1906 by Robert Hatcher. The Alaska Gold Quartz Mining Company staked its claims in 1907 but did not do any serious work until the late 1930s.

From 1937 until the mine was closed in 1942, the Independence Mine, with 200 employees, was one of the busiest mines in the district. The mining camp located below it had more than two dozen buildings, including an apartment house, two bunkhouses, a cookhouse/mess hall, a combination commissary/post office/mining office, an assay office, an electrical shop, a machine shop, a mill building, a powerhouse, a framing shop, stores of all kinds, and about 20 individual cabins for married miners and their families.

After the end of World War II, the mine reopened and operated until January 1951, when it shut down for good. In 1974, the historical value of the property was noted, and it was listed on the National Register of Historic Places. In 1980, the owners donated it to the state of Alaska, and Independence Mine State Historic Park was formed. Since then, some of the buildings have been restored, and others have been stabilized.

The northern portion of the mining camp includes a cluster of larger buildings. The first floor of the big, white, three-story building on the left housed the engineering offices and a warehouse (which stocked all the needed supplies for the crew). The second and third floors held bunk rooms, one of which was used as a school for a short time. The three-story building to the rear center was Bunkhouse #1, which was built in 1938 and housed 50 people. This building had electricity, plumbing, and heating. The smaller building in the center was a framing shop. Here large timbers were cut for mine supports. It also supplied lumber used for construction jobs around the camp.

**LEFT** These proud miners from the first half of the 1900s stand at a windlass, a winch used to lower and raise materials into and out of the mine.

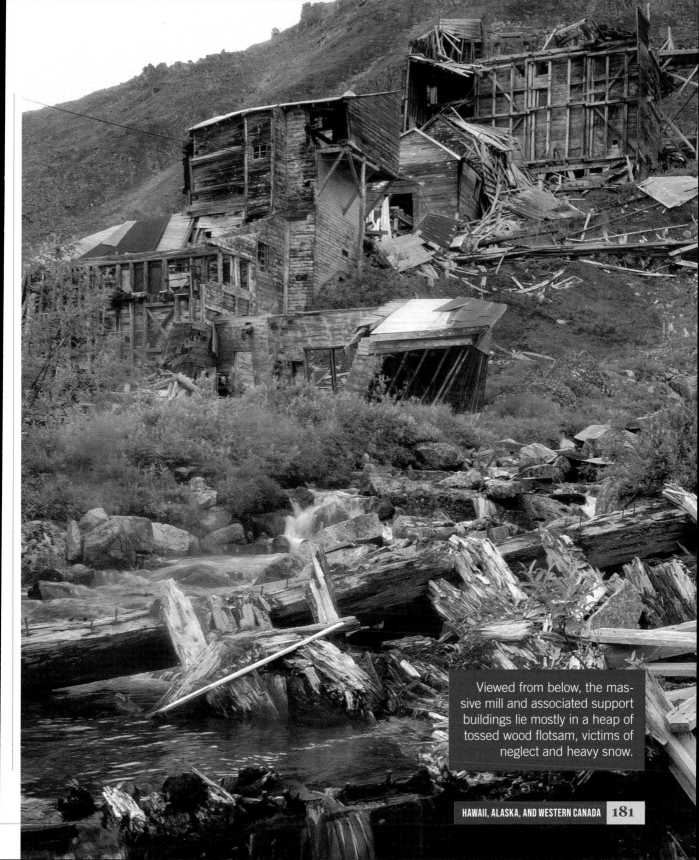

Viewed from below, the massive mill and associated support buildings lie mostly in a heap of tossed wood flotsam, victims of neglect and heavy snow.

# Kennicott, Alaska

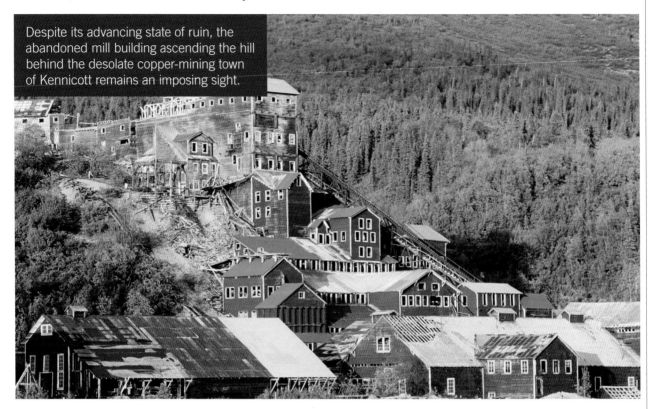

Despite its advancing state of ruin, the abandoned mill building ascending the hill behind the desolate copper-mining town of Kennicott remains an imposing sight.

**I**s it spelled with an *E* or an *I*? The parent company, Kennecott Mines Company, spells it with an *E*. The mining camp was named after a nearby glacier, which was named after naturalist and explorer Robert Kennicott, and is spelled with an *I*. Still in business and based in Utah, the Kennecott Mining Company was also named after him, even though it is spelled differently.

From 1906 through 1938, this copper mining town was located at the foot of the Wrangell Range in the south-east corner of non-panhandle Alaska, an isolated area. Mining began around 1906, and in 1908 the post office was established, along with a train to Cordova, the Copper River & North-western Railway. The mining camp had 494 people in 1920 and at its peak is said to have had 800 folks. As a remote company town, Kennicott had to be self-sufficient, so among its amenities were a hospital, a movie theater, a recreation hall, and a school. It also had a clean reputation with strict rules for citizens to follow. In December 1938, the post office closed, the residents boarded the last train out of Kennicott, and the town was abandoned.

In 1941, the Kennecott Company deeded the railroad to the state for use as a road. Except for a few curious and adventurous types who managed to work their way into town, the old mining camp sat vacant. Then in 1986, it was declared a national historic landmark. The National Park Service has come in and is in the process of restoring some of the 40 buildings that remain.

This July 1982 view of Kennicott's power plant building looks to the northeast. The plant supplied electrical power to the massive mill complex as well as to the town.

# Skagway, Alaska

A view of the wooden wharfs in Skagway Harbor lining across the mudflats in 1898.

They came, they saw, they went. Treasure seekers hustled off of all types of floating vessels that got them to the wooden docks extending out in the mudflats at Skagway. Bright lights, cards, booze, and female companionship beckoned, trying to separate them from what little money they had. Inflated prices and the Canadian requirement that miners carry massive supply loads slapped the new arrivals with reality. Skagway was willing to cooperate—for a price.

Established at the head of the Inside Passage, Skagway was not a mining town but was instead an outfitting center and gathering point for miners during the great Klondike Gold Rush of 1897–98. This was just the beginning of the grueling 450-mile overland trail to the Yukon's gold mines around Dawson City. Within a year of the first boat's landing in July

1897, Skagway had become Alaska's largest city, with upwards of 10,000 people. Gold, lawlessness, and anarchy made it famous, and tourism has kept it alive.

After the gold rush, Skagway faded but didn't die. In 1900, as many as 1,800 people remained, and the population has not ducked below 500 since. Gone were the boomers, gone were the saloons, and gone were the diversions. Post-boom Skagway capitalized on its location, remaining a shipping center for inland mines as well as being a popular cruise ship destination and tourist center. This quaint little town filled with Victorian buildings and 862 residents annually draws more than 900,000 folks looking to experience its colorful gold-rush past.

**ABOVE** In the "good old days" of the gold rush, Skagway's streets were an unending parade of miners heading off to the hinterlands. This was their last chance to stock up on the massive amounts of provisions required by Canadian officials before entering Canada.

**BELOW** These restored buildings are part of Skagway's "Old Town."

# Dawson City, Yukon Territory

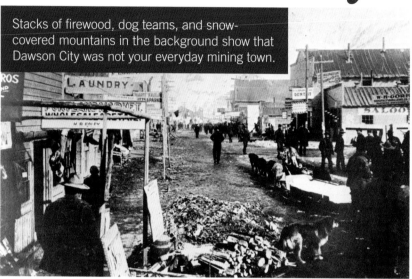

Stacks of firewood, dog teams, and snow-covered mountains in the background show that Dawson City was not your everyday mining town.

It has been called the Last Great Gold Rush. In August 1896, gold was discovered near the confluence of the Klondike and Yukon rivers in the heart of Canada's Yukon Territory, seemingly a gazillion miles from anywhere and everywhere. Once word hit Seattle in the summer of 1897, as many as 100,000 starry-eyed miners and wannabe miners converged to this point on the Yukon River. Unfortunately for them, all the best locations had already been staked, and mining had commenced. They persisted, however, and the summers of 1897 and 1898 were like the California Gold Rush revisited.

Most came by sea through Skagway and its neighboring town of Dyea, so after the brutal 450-mile journey to Dawson City, they had to make the best of the situation. Dawson blossomed in the long summer days, and soon some 25,000 to 40,000 people called it home. Grand Forks, ten miles south on Bonanza Creek, had 10,000 residents.

Neither of those numbers includes the thousands living outside the grasp of those two towns. By 1898, Dawson had reached its peak and had bustling suburbs at Klondike City and Grand Forks.

Dawson City was no shrinking violet and gave Skagway a run for its money on prices, vices, and corruption. The flush years didn't last long, however. By 1899 the

Ripped apart by four fires in its first four years and built alongside the Yukon River on permafrost, Dawson City still lives on. The miners are mostly gone, as are the stacks of firewood and the dog teams.

A bakery and ice cream shop decorate restored, painted storefronts of today's Dawson City. A deep pride of the past and a tough development policy, as well as a town ordinance that requires all new or remodeled buildings to be built in the style of the old town, keeps the community looking similar to the way it did more than 100 years ago.

population had dropped by 8,000, and then to 5,000 by the time Dawson incorporated in 1902. In 2016, the census counted 1,375 people, most earning their living mining gold or catering to the 60,000 tourists a year that explore its historic streets

# Barkerville, British Columbia

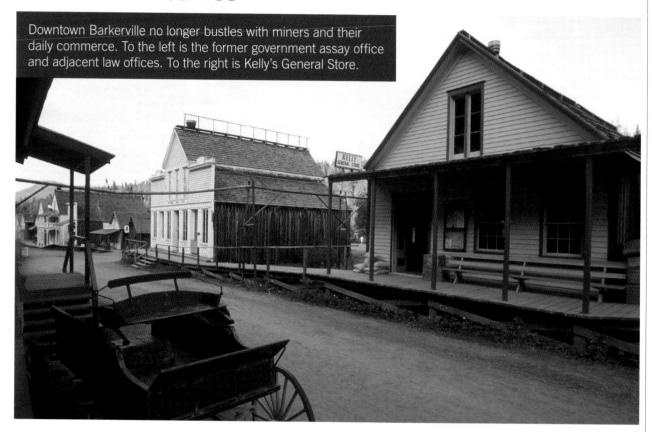

Downtown Barkerville no longer bustles with miners and their daily commerce. To the left is the former government assay office and adjacent law offices. To the right is Kelly's General Store.

On the Cariboo Wagon Road, deep in the heart of British Columbia—95 miles east of Quensel and southeast of Prince George—is the magnificent, restored ghost town of Barkerville. Billy Barker discovered gold on Williams Creek in 1862, and thousands of miners descended into the area around his claims. By the next summer, hotels, restaurants, cafés, saloons, dance halls, a church, a barbershop, and a multitude of stores lined the long main street of the new town of Barkerville, and some 10,000 people swarmed its sidewalks and streets.

**ABOVE** The old stove inside this Barkerville cabin probably spent many winter days glowing nearly red to beat back the heavy, damp cold of British Columbia's interior winter weather.

**BELOW** This photo was taken on Dominion Day, now called Canada Day, July 1, 1871. The Barkerville library is on the left, with John and Emily Bowron standing out front. Next door, Mr. and Mrs. William Davison stand in the doorway of their grocery store. Note the elevated sidewalk.

But the compact wooden town was a fire waiting to happen. In September 1868, the wait was over. After the fire, Barkerville was quickly rebuilt—in wood—but with space for cross streets.

Barkerville was not a violent town, despite the gin mills, dance halls, and other such diversions. But by 1870, the end was near. As gold production decreased, other new booms elsewhere caught the attention of the miners, who abandoned Barkerville for more enticing opportunities.

In 1957, the province of British Columbia purchased this property and began to restore its buildings. Today, more than 125 buildings have been renewed, giving Barkerville a second life as a living history museum.

# The Drumheller Valley, Alberta

In 1952, a cable ferry still carried cars across the Red Deer River. Dorothy and a pair of grain elevators are visible on the far side of the river.

**T**he Drumheller Valley, 75 miles northeast of Calgary, is the heart of Alberta's badlands, a dry rolling landscape loaded with hoodoos, coulees, and numerous ghost and semi-ghost towns.

Two churches were established here, about a hundred yards apart, a United church and Catholic church. Shown here is the Catholic church through the window of the United church building. Restoration of both buildings by the Dorothy Historical Society commenced around 2006 and is still ongoing.

work progressed the [coal] seam ran poorly as there was too much bone in the coal." Those bones were dinosaur bones! Wayne's buildings include the well-preserved Rosedeer Hotel and Last Chance Saloon.

Established in 1928, East Coulee only has about 5 percent of the population it had in the 1930s. Its coal mines closed by the late 1940s. A tad down the road from there is Dorothy. The Dorothy post office opened in this tiny agricultural community in 1908, and by the 1920s the railroad had come. Dorothy boasted of three grain elevators, a church, a school, a restaurant, a butcher shop, a pool room, and three stores all to serve the less than 100 residents. Most of those buildings remain—empty.

Cambria and Wayne are the shriveled remains of neighboring coal towns

from the era between 1910 and 1940. At Cambria, a sign tells the story: "As

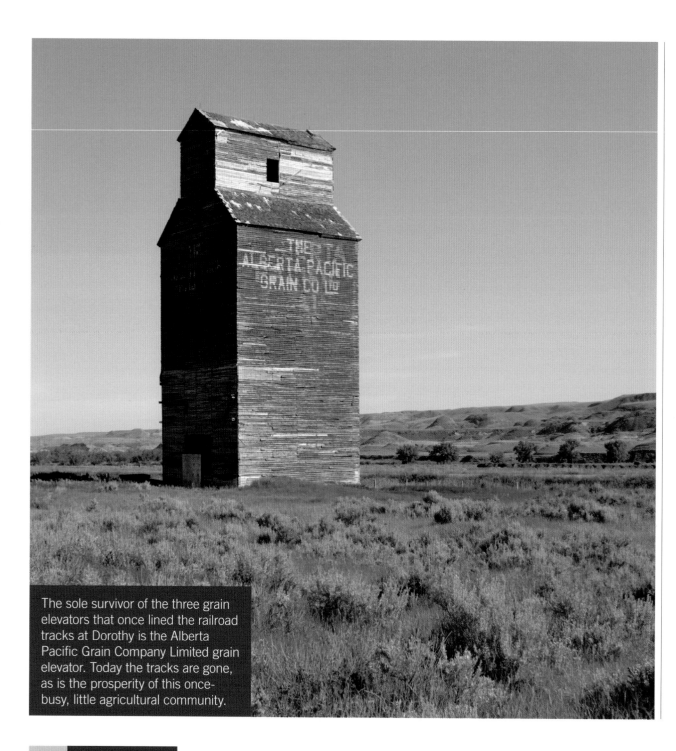

The sole survivor of the three grain elevators that once lined the railroad tracks at Dorothy is the Alberta Pacific Grain Company Limited grain elevator. Today the tracks are gone, as is the prosperity of this once-busy, little agricultural community.